How to

Make an

LL

HOW TO
MAKE AN
ILLINOIS WILL

Third Edition

Diana Brodman Summers
Mark Warda
Attorneys at Law

SPHINX® PUBLISHING
AN IMPRINT OF SOURCEBOOKS, INC.®
NAPERVILLE, ILLINOIS

Third Edition, 2002

Published by: **Sphinx® Publishing, An Imprint of Sourcebooks, Inc.®**

<u>Naperville Office</u>
P.O. Box 4410
Naperville, Illinois 60567-4410
630-961-3900
Fax: 630-961-2168
http://www.sourcebooks.com
http://www.sphinxlegal.com

This publication is designed to provide accurate and authoritative information in regard to the subject matter covered. It is sold with the understanding that the publisher is not engaged in rendering legal, accounting, or other professional service. If legal advice or other expert assistance is required, the services of a competent professional person should be sought.

From a Declaration of Principles Jointly Adopted by a Committee of the
American Bar Association and a Committee of Publishers and Associations

This product is not a substitute for legal advice.
Disclaimer required by Texas statutes.

Library of Congress Cataloging-in-Publication Data
Summers, Diana Brodman.
    How to make an Illinois will / Diana Brodman Summers, Mark Warda.-- 3rd ed.
        p. cm. -- (Legal survival guides)
    Includes index.
    ISBN 1-57248-170-6 (alk. paper)
    1. Wills--Illinois--Popular works. I. Warda, Mark. II. Title. III. Series.

KFI1344.Z9 S86 2002
346.77305'4--dc21

                                                                        2001048353

Printed and bound in the United States of America.
VHG Paperback — 10 9 8 7 6 5 4 3 2 1

CONTENTS

USING SELF-HELP LAW BOOKS

Before using a self-help law book, you should realize the advantages and disadvantages of doing your own legal work and understand the challenges and diligence that this requires.

THE GROWING TREND

Rest assured that you won't be the first or only person handling your own legal matter. For example, in some states, more than seventy-five percent of divorces and other cases have at least one party representing him or herself. Because of the high cost of legal services, this is a major trend and many courts are struggling to make it easier for people to represent themselves. However, some courts are not happy with people who do not use attorneys and refuse to help them in any way. For some, the attitude is, "Go to the law library and figure it out for yourself."

We at Sphinx write and publish self-help law books to give people an alternative to the often complicated and confusing legal books found in most law libraries. We have made the explanations of the law as simple and easy to understand as possible. Of course, unlike an attorney advising an individual client, we cannot cover every conceivable possibility.

COST/VALUE ANALYSIS

Whenever you shop for a product or service, you are faced with various levels of quality and price. In deciding what product or service to buy, you make a cost/value analysis on the basis of your willingness to pay and the quality you desire.

When buying a car, you decide whether you want transportation, comfort, status, or sex appeal. Accordingly, you decide among such choices as a Neon, a Lincoln, a Rolls Royce, or a Porsche. Before making a decision, you usually weigh the merits of each option against the cost.

When you get a headache, you can take a pain reliever (such as aspirin) or visit a medical specialist for a neurological examination. Given this choice, most people, of course, take a pain reliever, since it costs only pennies; whereas a medical examination costs hundreds of dollars and takes a lot of time. This is usually a logical choice because it is rare to need anything more than a pain reliever for a headache. But in some cases, a headache may indicate a brain tumor and failing to see a specialist right away can result in complications. Should everyone with a headache go to a specialist? Of course not, but people treating their own illnesses must realize that they are betting on the basis of their cost/value analysis of the situation. They are taking the most logical option.

The same cost/value analysis must be made when deciding to do one's own legal work. Many legal situations are very straight forward, requiring a simple form and no complicated analysis. Anyone with a little intelligence and a book of instructions can handle the matter without outside help.

But there is always the chance that complications are involved that only an attorney would notice. To simplify the law into a book like this, several legal cases often must be condensed into a single sentence or paragraph. Otherwise, the book would be several hundred pages long and too complicated for most people. However, this simplification necessarily leaves out many details and nuances that would apply to special or unusual situations. Also, there are many ways to interpret most legal questions. Your case may come before a judge who disagrees with the analysis of our authors.

Therefore, in deciding to use a self-help law book and to do your own legal work, you must realize that you are making a cost/value analysis. You have decided that the money you will save in doing it yourself outweighs the chance that your case will not turn out to your satisfaction. Most people handling their own simple legal matters never have a problem, but occasionally people find that it ended up costing them more to have an attorney straighten out the situation than it would have if they had hired an attorney in the beginning. Keep this in mind if you decide to handle your own case, and be sure to consult an attorney if you feel you might need further guidance.

LOCAL RULES   The next thing to remember is that a book which covers the law for the entire nation, or even for an entire state, cannot possibly include every procedural difference of every county court. Whenever possible, we provide the exact form needed; however, in some areas, each county, or even each judge, may require unique forms and procedures. In our *state* books, our forms usually cover the majority of counties in the state, or provide examples of the type of form that will be required. In our *national* books, our forms are sometimes even more general in nature but are designed to give a good idea of the type of form that will be needed in most locations. Nonetheless, keep in mind that your *state*, county, or judge may have a requirement, or use a form, that is not included in this book.

You should not necessarily expect to be able to get all of the information and resources you need solely from within the pages of this book. This book will serve as your guide, giving you specific information whenever possible and helping you to find out what else you will need to know. This is just like if you decided to build your own backyard deck. You might purchase a book on how to build decks. However, such a book would not include the building codes and permit requirements of every city, town, county, and township in the nation; nor would it include the lumber, nails, saws, hammers, and other materials and tools you would need to actually build the deck. You would use the book as your guide, and then do some work and research involving such matters as whether you need a permit of some kind, what type and grade of wood are available in your area, whether to use hand tools or power tools, and how to use those tools.

Before using the forms in a book like this, you should check with your court clerk to see if there are any local rules of which you should be aware, or local forms you will need to use. Often, such forms will require the same information as the forms in the book but are merely laid out differently, use slightly different language, or use different color paper so the clerks can easily find them. They will sometimes require additional information.

CHANGES IN THE LAW

Besides being subject to state and local rules and practices, the law is subject to change at any time. The courts and the legislatures of all fifty states are constantly revising the laws. It is possible that while you are reading this book, some aspect of the law is being changed or that a court is interpreting a law in a different way. You should always check the most recent statutes, rules and regulations to see what, if any changes have been made.

In most cases, the change will be of minimal significance. A form will be redesigned, additional information will be required, or a waiting period will be extended. As a result, you might need to revise a form, file an extra form, or wait out a longer time period; these types of changes will not usually affect the outcome of your case. On the other hand, sometimes a major part of the law is changed, the entire law in a particular area is rewritten, or a case that was the basis of a central legal point is overruled. In such instances, your entire ability to pursue your case may be impaired.

Again, you should weigh the value of your case against the cost of an attorney and make a decision as to what you believe is in your best interest.

INTRODUCTION

This book is intended to give Illinois residents a basic understanding of the laws regarding wills, joint property, and other types of ownership of property as they affect their estate planning. It is designed to allow those with simple estates to quickly and inexpensively set up their affairs to distribute their property according to their wishes.

It also includes information on appointing a guardian for minor children. This can be useful in avoiding bad feelings between relatives and in protecting the children from being raised by someone you would object to.

Chapter 1 provides general information on making a will, how to work with an estate planning attorney, an introduction to Illinois estate planning laws, and where to get additional information. Chapter 2 explains specific examples of will clauses and their effect on your estate. Chapter 3 covers the reasons for having a will, and Chapter 4 is a brief introduction to the legal system of probate.

Chapter 5 explains each section of a simple will in depth. Chapter 6 will walk you through the procedure for signing your will. Chapter 7 explains how to change, cancel, and store your will. Chapter 8 and Chapter 9 explain the Advance Directives of a *Living Will* and a *Health Care Power of Attorney*, documents which protect a person when they are too ill to speak for themselves.

Chapter 10 discusses another common legal document the *Property Power of Attorney*, while Chapter 11 lists ways to make anatomical gifts. Chapter 12 is a brief introduction to trusts, and Chapter 13 briefly recounts the steps to take beyond your will.

The Glossary lists commonly used legal terms regarding wills and estate planning. You may wish to review the glossary prior to reading the rest of this book.

Appendix A contains some sample filled-in will forms to show you how it is done. Appendix B contains blank will forms you can tear out or photocopy.

You can prepare your own will quickly and easily by using the forms out of the book, by photocopying them, or you can retype the material on blank paper. The small amount of time it takes to do this can give you and your heirs the peace of mind of knowing that your estate will be distributed according to your wishes.

A surprising number of people have had their estates pass to the wrong parties because of a simple lack of knowledge of what they were doing. Before using any of the forms in Appendix B, you should read and understand the previous chapters of this book.

In each example given you might ask, "What if my spouse dies first?" or "What if my children are grown?" and then the answer might be different. If your situation is at all complicated you are advised to seek the advice of an attorney. In many communities wills are available for very reasonable prices. No book of this type can cover every contingency in every case, but a knowledge of the basics will help you to make the right decisions regarding your property.

GENERAL
CONSIDERATIONS

1

Whether you are planning on making your own will, plan to use an attorney to assist you in creating an estate plan, or just want to gather more information on the subject of estate documents and wills in Illinois, the first step should be to review Chapters 1 through 13. If you are planning to write your own will, it may be helpful to locate the forms in the back of this book now so you can refer to the particular forms while reading the chapters.

This book also contains several definitions that will be helpful in understanding the legal terms used both in this book and in speaking with an attorney. Please refer to the Glossary at the back of this book.

PREPARING TO MAKE A WILL

Whether you create your own will or have an attorney prepare one as part of your estate plan, there are preliminary things that you will need to do. The first step is to take an inventory of all your assets. While this may seem overwhelming, the best way is to start by listing broad categories of items such as; stocks and bonds, insurance policies, bank accounts, real property (home, land), jewelry, auto, collectibles, etc. Once you start with the broad categories, break them down into exact items. Remember that in a will you do NOT have to list everything of value because any property not mentioned in the list will be taken care of by a *residuary clause*.

Example: "All the rest, residue and remainder of my estate, real or personal, wheresoever situate, now owned or hereafter acquired by me, which at the time of my death shall belong to me or be subject to my disposal, I give, devise and bequeath unto my son Theodore Joseph Summers. If my said son does not survive me, I give, and bequeath said property to my niece Heather Summers and her descendants, per stirpes."

Next, you should determine your objectives in preparing a will. Are you concerned about passing property to heirs in the most tax efficient manner? Do you need to provide for someone who is disabled? Do you wish to give certain items to specific heirs? Your objectives will determine not only the wording of your will but whether you should get an attorney to help you create an estate plan.

The last part of preparation is to make a list of family members and beneficiaries. Consider what you would want to leave to your family members.

There are worksheets in Appendix B of this book that will help you organize your thoughts in order to prepare your will. There is an ASSET AND BENEFICIARY LIST. (see form 1, p.95.) There is also a PREFERENCES LIST. (see form 2, p.99.)

USING AN ATTORNEY

If your goal is to create an estate plan instead of a simple will, whether it be because of special circumstances, complexities of your situation, or because you want additional estate documents, you should consult an attorney who is familiar with estate planning.

Choosing an attorney can be confusing. Many people rely on referrals from family, friends, or business associates such as your investment broker, insurance broker, or bank. You can also obtain referrals from local county or state bar associations. Whatever way you select an attorney to assist you in creating an estate plan, make sure that this attorney is familiar with the complex and rapidly changing area of estate planning law.

COSTS AND FEES

Many people shy away from using an attorney due to the costs of legal services. However there are ways to keep costs down and still get the needed services. The first step, of course, is to shop around for an attorney who meets your legal and financial criteria. This may require calls to several law firms inquiring about their services, their experience in estate planning, and their costs.

Another way to keep costs down is to be prepared for all meetings with your attorney. Do not wait until the last minute to gather information on your estate, copies of documents, or a list a questions for your meetings with your attorney. A client who comes prepared to meetings with information, writes down several questions before calling their attorney, and promptly provides documents when asked to do so, conveys the message that they will not pay for wasted time.

WORKSHEETS AND INFORMATION

Some estate planning attorneys will send a client an estate planning worksheet to fill out prior to their first meeting. Others rely on information gathered at meetings. If your attorney sends you a form to fill out make sure the form is completed on time and that the information you provide is accurate. You may also want to bring the ASSET & BENEFICIARY LIST (form 1) and the PREFERENCE LIST (form 2) in Appendix B of this book, with you to your first meeting with your attorney.

Other information you will be asked for:

- spouse's: name, date of birth, if deceased date of death, if divorced date of divorce;

- children: name, date of birth, if deceased date of death, name of their spouses and children;

- members of family requiring long term medical care; or

- if you have lived or have property in a community property state (Arizona, California, Idaho, Louisiana, Nevada, New Mexico, Texas, or Washington).

Documents you may want to bring to your first meeting with your estate planning attorney are:

- copies of current or prior wills, trusts, powers of attorney;

- a financial statement summary show debts and assets;

- copies of deeds to property;

- retirement benefit summary;

- life insurance information;

- stock or other business interests;

- pre-nuptial agreements; and

- an outline of your family tree.

THE LAW

Illinois has several statutes that cover wills and probate. The primary one is Chapter 755 of the Illinois Complied Statutes. This chapter includes the Probate Act, Safety Deposit Box Opening Act, Lifetime Transfer of Property Act, Living Will Act, Power of Attorney Act, and other laws that concern the planning of and the probating of an estate. Chapter 760 covers Trusts and their administration.

Most people find the wording of these laws tedious and vague. If your estate plan is so complex that you are attempting to read these statutes, that is probably a sign that you need to get the help of an experienced estate planning attorney.

SOURCES OF INFORMATION

The Internet has become a valuable source of information in our society. There are many sites, which are directed at increasing the public's knowledge of estate documents. Many of the bar associations provide links to information sites as does several of the government sites.

However, there are problems with Internet sites. There is no guarantee that the information posted is correct or even the current law. Also, no Internet site can answer all your questions on making a will. That personalized service can only be obtained from an attorney who is familiar with the creation of estate documents.

The following Internet sites have been around for some time and should be reliable places to begin research. These sites provide links to several additional sources of information and points of research. Remember you can always do an Internet search on words like "Illinois will," "estate planning," or other more specific terms.

American Bar Association:

> http://www.abanet.org

DuPage County Bar Association:

> http://www.dcba.org

Illinois State Bar Association:

> http://www.isba.org

Legal Research: www.findlaw.com:

> http://www.lawguru.com

Federal Legal Research:

> http://www.fedlaw.gsa.gov
> http://www.firstgov.gov

Social Security:

> http://www.ssa.gov

KNOWING THE BASIC RULES 2

Before making your will, you should understand how a will works and what it can and cannot do. Otherwise, your plans may not be carried out and the wrong people may end up with your property.

WILLS DEFINED

A *will* is a document you can use to control who gets your property, who will be guardian of your children and their property, and who will manage your estate after your death.

The basic elements of a will are:

- your name and address;

- names of spouse, children, and other beneficiaries;

- alternate beneficiaries;

- description of assets;

- specific gifts to specific beneficiaries;

- name of executor and an alternate executor;

- name of guardian and an alternate guardian;

- your signature; and

- witnesses' signatures.

How a Will Is Used

Some people think a will avoids *probate*. It does not.

NOTE: *Probate is a generic term that is commonly used to mean the filing of a will with what is called a probate court and the payment of taxes on an estate. The technical legal definition of probate is a court procedure by which a will is proven to be valid and the directives expressed in the will are carried out, within the law.*

A will is the document used in probate to determine who receives the property and who is appointed guardian and executor or personal representative. The filing of a will in the probate court is governed by state law. Probate can be beneficial to the heirs by providing court supervision in the distribution of assets and adherence to the terms of the will. (See Chapter 4 for an explanation of probate.)

Avoiding
Probate

If you wish to avoid probate, you need to use methods other than a will, such as joint ownership, pay-on-death accounts, or living trusts. Joint ownership and pay-on-death accounts are discussed later in this chapter. For information on living trusts you should refer to a book which focuses on trusts as used for estate planning.

Everyone should have a will in case some property, which was forgotten or received just prior to death, does not avoid probate for some reason; or if both husband and wife die at the same time.

Joint Tenancy and Probate

Property that is owned in *joint tenancy with right of survivorship* does not pass under a will. If a will gives the property to one person but it is already in a joint account with another person, the will is usually ignored and the joint owner of the account gets the property. This is because the property in the account avoids probate and passes directly to the joint owner. A will only controls property that goes through probate. If money is put into a joint account only for convenience, it might pass under the will; but if the joint owner does not give it up, it could take an expensive court battle to get it back.

Putting property into joint tenancy does not give absolute rights to it. If the estate owes estate taxes, the recipient of joint tenancy property may have to contribute to the tax payment. Also, some states give spouses a right to property that is in joint accounts with other people. This is explained later in this chapter.

Example 1: Ted and his wife want all of their property to go to the survivor of them. They put their house, cars, bank accounts, and brokerage accounts in joint ownership. When Ted dies, his wife only has to show his death certificate to get all the property transferred to her name. No probate or will is necessary.

Example 2: After Ted's death, his wife, Michelle puts all of the property and accounts into joint ownership with her son, Mark. Upon her death, Mark needs only to present her death certificate to have everything transferred into his name. No probate or will is necessary.

JOINT TENANCY AND YOUR WILL

If all property is in joint ownership or if all property is distributed through a will, things are simple. But when some property passes by each method, a person's plans may not be fulfilled.

Example 1: Bill's will leaves all his property to his wife, Mary. Bill dies owning a house jointly with his sister, Joan, and a bank account jointly with his son, Don. Upon Bill's death, Joan gets the house, Don gets the bank account and his wife, Mary, gets nothing.

Example 2: Betty's will leaves half her assets to Ann and half her assets to George. Betty dies owning $1,000,000 in stock jointly with George and a car in her own name. Ann gets only a half interest in the car. George gets all the stock and a half interest in the car.

Example 3: John's will leaves all his property equally to his five children. Before going in the hospital he puts his oldest son, Harry, as a joint owner of his accounts. John dies and Harry gets all of his assets. The rest of the children get nothing.

In each of these cases the property went to a person it probably should not have because the decedent did not realize that joint ownership overruled their will. In some families this might not be a problem. Harry might divide the property equally (and possibly pay a gift tax). But in many cases Harry would just keep everything and the family would never talk to him again, or would take him to court for an expensive legal battle.

JOINT TENANCY AND RISKS

In many cases it may appear that joint tenancy is the ideal way to own property, but it often creates even more problems. If you put your real estate in joint ownership with someone, you cannot sell it or mortgage it without that person's signature. If you put your bank account in joint ownership with someone, they can withdraw all of the money in that account.

Example 1: Alice put her house in joint ownership with her son. She later married Ed and moved in with him. She wanted to sell her house and to invest the money for income. Her son refused to sign the deed. She was in court for ten months getting her house back and the judge almost refused to do it.

Example 2: Alex put his bank accounts into joint ownership with his daughter Mary to avoid probate. Mary fell in love with Doug who was in trouble with the law. Doug talked Mary into "borrowing" $30,000 from the account for a "business deal" that went sour. Later she "borrowed" $25,000 more to pay Doug's bail bond. Alex did not find out until it was too late that his money was gone.

"Tenancy in Common" and Probate

In Illinois, there are three basic ways to own property: joint tenancy with right of survivorship, tenancy in common, and tenancy by the entirety.

Joint tenancy with right of survivorship means when one owner of the property dies the survivor automatically gets the decedent's share. *Tenancy in common* means when one owner dies, that owner's share of the property goes to his or her heirs under the will. Probate is *not* avoided. A *tenancy by the entirety* is like joint tenancy with right of survivorship, but it can only apply to a married couple.

Example 1: Tom and Marcia bought a house and lived together for twenty years, but were never married. The deed did not specify joint tenancy. When Tom died, his brother inherited his half of the house and it had to be sold because Marcia could not afford to buy it from him.

Example 2: Lindsay and her husband Rocky bought a house. When Rocky suddenly died, Lindsay obtained full ownership of the house by filing a death certificate at the courthouse. That was because the deed to the house stated that they were husband and wife so ownership was presumed to be tenancy by the entirety.

Your Spouse

Under Illinois law, a surviving spouse can elect to take a portion of the decedent's estate no matter what the person's will states. This is true even if the surviving spouse is not mentioned in the will. The surviving spouse can get one-third of the entire estate if there are descendants and one-half of the entire estate if there are no descendants. The surviving spouse must file a *renunciation* of the will in court in order to overrule the will. This is sometimes called an *elective share* or a *forced share*.

The state law does not required use of a specific form to renounce a share of a will. Before deciding to file a renunciation you may wish to consult with an attorney or a financial advisor because of the effect this may have on taxes and your estate. The reason behind this law is to protect the surviving spouse who has not worked outside the home throughout the marriage.

Example 1: John's will leaves all of his property to his children of a prior marriage and nothing to his current wife. At John's death, his wife can elect to renounce the will and get one-third of John's estate. The children would then divide the remaining two-thirds of John's estate.

Example 2: Mary puts her money in a joint account with her husband. In her will, Mary leaves all of her other property to her neighbor. Neither John nor Mary have any descendants. When she dies, Mary's husband gets all the money in the joint account, and if he elects to renounce Mary's will, one-half of all her other property.

A SPOUSE'S SHARE

While some feel it is wrong to avoid giving a spouse the share allowed by law, there are legitimate reasons for doing so (such as where there are children from a prior marriage). The law allows some exceptions.

In Illinois, a spouse's share may be avoided by owning property in joint tenancy with someone else or putting the property in a trust for someone else. You may also avoid the spouse's share if your spouse signs a written agreement giving up his or her rightful share. This agreement can be signed either before or after the marriage. Another way to leave something to someone other than you spouse is with a life insurance policy naming someone other than your spouse as beneficiary.

However, your spouse may have a change of mind when they find that they are receiving little or nothing from your estate and then file a will contest suit. When faced with such a suit from the spouse, most courts will look at the spouse's ability to earn a living, any dependent children, if the spouse's share was given up in a legal procedure, and other aspects of the estate. Remember, any will contest suit is costly for the heirs and may negate any monetary benefit they might have received from the estate.

Avoiding a spouse's share, especially without his or her knowledge, opens the possibility of a lawsuit after your death, and if your actions were not done to precise legal requirements they could be thrown out. Therefore, you should consider consulting an attorney if you plan to leave your spouse less than the share provided by law.

I/T/F BANK ACCOUNTS VERSUS JOINT OWNERSHIP

One way of keeping bank accounts out of your estate and still retain control is to title them *in trust for* or I/T/F and naming a beneficiary. Some banks may use the letters POD for *pay on death* or TOD for *transfer on death*. Either way the result is the same. No one except you can get the money until your death, and on death it immediately goes directly to the person you name without a will or probate proceeding. These are what are called *Totten trusts* after the court case that declared them legal.

Example: Rich opened a bank account in the name of "Rich, I/T/F Mary." If Rich dies, the money automatically goes to Mary. Prior to Rich's death, Mary has no control over the account, she doesn't even have to know about it, and Rich can take Mary's name off the account at any time.

Securities Registered as I/T/F

The drawback of the Totten trust has been that it is only good for cash in a bank account. Stocks and bonds still had to go through probate. But in 1995 the Illinois legislature passed a law allowing stocks, bonds, and securities accounts also to transfer automatically on death. Now an estate with cash and securities can pass on death with no need for court proceedings.

To set up your securities to transfer automatically on death, you need to have them correctly registered. If you use a brokerage account, the brokerage company should have a form for you to do this. If they do not have such a form or do not know about this law you should suggest that they check with their attorney about Illinois Statutes, Chapter 815, ILCS 10, or else move your account to another broker.

If your securities are registered in your own name or with your spouse, you need to reregister them with a designation of beneficiary. The following illustrations of how to do so are contained in Illinois Statutes, Chapter 815, ILCS Section 10/10:

Sole owner with sole beneficiary:

```
John S Brown TOD John S Brown Jr.
```

Multiple owners with sole beneficiary:

```
John S Brown, Mary B Brown JT TEN TOD John S
Brown Jr
```

Multiple owners-substituted beneficiary:

```
John S Brown, Mary B Brown JT TEN TOD John S
Brown Jr SUB BENE Peter Q Brown
```

Multiple owners-lineal descendants:

```
John S Brown, Mary B Brown JT TEN TOD John S
Brown Jr LDPS
```

WILLS AND YOUR HOMESTEAD

There are several meanings for the word *homestead* in Illinois. The most common one is the property tax exemption given to senior citizens who have owned and lived in a residence for a period of time. Other meanings have to do with additional tax exemptions, but these have nothing to do with whether the property is a homestead for estate purposes.

Illinois law defines a homestead for estate purposes as a $7,500 - exemption for property owned by a resident of Illinois in his or her name only at the time of death. This exemption applies to the surviving spouse and to any minor children, as long as they continue to occupy the homestead.

If your property is covered under the Illinois homestead exemption, your will has no control over it. Upon your death, your homestead automatically passes as follows:

- your spouse gets the right to occupy the homestead until his or her death;

- your minor children get the right to occupy the homestead until the youngest child becomes eighteen years old.

Whether or not a home is legally a homestead is a tricky legal question. It may depend on which spouse is providing the support or whether or not the property is also being used for business purposes. If you have a question of whether your property is a homestead for estate purposes, you should consult a lawyer who is experienced in estate planning.

Because homestead property can only be property that is in individual ownership, jointly held property and property in trust does not come under these rules. To avoid property becoming homestead property, it must be purchased in joint names or in trust. If it is already in an individual's name, it cannot be put in trust or in joint ownership without the spouse's signature.

It is possible to set up the title to your home in such a way that it will not be homestead and your spouse cannot claim an interest in it (for example if you want it to go to your children by a previous marriage). However, this should be done by a lawyer who is familiar with the latest cases in this area. If it is not done correctly, it may be thrown out by a court. In such a situation, you should also consider a written agreement with your spouse regarding the home.

EXCEPTIONS

Illinois law allows both spouse and child awards. The spouse's award is given to the surviving spouse of an Illinois resident. The spouse's award can be money or personal property of the deceased that will allow for proper support of the surviving spouse for nine months after the death of the decedent. The amount of money or value of personal property can be no less than $10,000. This award can be avoided if the will has a provision that clearly states that it is in lieu of the Illinois spouse's award.

The child's award is for minor or adult dependent children. Like the spouse's award, it can be money or personal property that allows for the proper support of the child for nine months after the death of the decedent. The amount of the child's award is no less than $5,000 per child. In both cases, the dollar amount of the award can be increased by the court.

Additionally, an estate may qualify as a *small estate*. A small estate is one that does not total more than $50,000. When adding up property of a small estate, do not include real property or bank accounts that are held in joint tenancy or *in trust for*. (See prior sections on page 14 for an explanation of these terms.) In a small estate, the surviving spouse gets the $10,000 award and the minor children or adult dependent children get the $5,000 each award, as explained in the previous paragraph. A Small Estate Affidavit may be required and should be drawn up by a qualified attorney.

MARRIAGE AND YOUR WILL

If you get married after making your will and do not rewrite it after the wedding, your spouse can get a share of your estate unless:

- you have a prenuptial agreement;

- you made a provision for your spouse in the will; or

- you stated in the will that you intended not to mention your prospective spouse.

Example: John made out his will leaving everything to his disabled brother. When he married Joan, an heiress with plenty of money, he didn't change his will because he still wanted his brother to get his estate. When he died Joan filed papers to renounce John's will. With court approval, Joan will get half of John's estate and his brother will get half.

DIVORCE AND YOUR WILL

In Illinois, getting divorced automatically deletes your former spouse's share from your will. Per Illinois Statute divorce revokes every "legacy or interest or power of appointment" given to the former spouse. (Ill. Stat.755 ILCS, Sec. 5/4-7(b).) The will takes effect as if the former spouse has died first. However, a new will should be made at the time of a divorce because your former spouse may try to get a share of the estate just because he or she is mentioned in the will. A suit from the former spouse may cost your estate considerable legal fees just to defeat the claim.

Example: George and Eunice made their wills leaving half their property to each other and half to their children from their previous marriages. George and Eunice divorced, but after the divorce, George forgot to make a new will. When George died, Eunice hired a lawyer to file papers claiming half the estate.

The lawyer representing George's children pointed out that Eunice should not get a share of the estate because of the divorce. However, Eunice demanded a trial, hoping the children would settle the case by giving her a few thousand dollars. They refused to settle but their attorney charged $5,000 for the trial.

If you do not have time to make a new will immediately after your divorce, you may want to revoke your old will. This can be done by tearing it up or by other ways discussed in Chapter 7. By revoking your will you are choosing to use your state's distribution system of deciding yours heirs (which, in Illinois, does not include your former spouse).

CHILDREN AND YOUR WILL

If you have a child after making your will and you do not rewrite your will, the child gets a share of your estate as if there was no will. However the size of the share may not be what you planned.

Example: Dave who has no spouse, made a will leaving half his estate to his sister and the other half to be shared by his three children. He later has another child and does not revise his will. Upon his death his fourth child would get one quarter of his estate, his sister would get three-eighths and the other three children would each get one-eighth.

It is best to rewrite your will at the birth of a child. However, another solution is to include the following clause after the names of your children in your will.

> "...and any afterborn children living at the time of my death in equal shares."

Be warned, this type of clause may open up your estate for claims from those who claim to be children, merely to get part of the estate. This is especially true for large estates and estates of the rich and famous.

YOUR DEBTS

One of the duties of the person administering an estate (an *executor*) is to pay the debts of the decedent. Before an estate is distributed to the heirs, the legitimate debts must be ascertained and paid. This includes debts incurred from the funeral of the decedent.

An exception is *secured debts*. These are debts that are protected by a lien against property, like a home loan or a car loan. In the case of a secured debt, the loan does not have to be paid before the property is distributed.

Example: John owns a $100,000 house with a $80,000 mortgage and he has $100,000. Upon his death, if he leaves the house to his brother and the bank account to his sister, then his brother would get the home but would owe the $80,000 mortgage.

What if your debts are more than your property? Today, unlike hundreds of years ago, people cannot inherit other peoples' debts. A person's property is used to pay their probate and funeral expenses first, and if there is not enough left to pay their other debts, then the creditors are out of luck. However, if a person leaves property to people and does not have enough assets to pay his or her debts, then the property will be sold to pay the debts.

Example: Jeb's will leaves all of his property to his three children. At the time of his death, Jeb has $300,000 in medical bills, $11,000 in credit card debt, and his only assets are his car and $5,000 in stock. The car and stock will be sold and the funeral bill and probate fees paid out of the proceeds. If any money is left it goes to the creditors, and in this case, probably nothing is left for the children. However, the children may not have to pay the medical bills or credit card debt as long as they did not co-sign or legally assume these debts of their father.

NOTE: *Many creditors will go to great lengths to prove that the family of the deceased is liable for the outstanding bills. This is especially true when the family does receive some property from the will. The family may consider taking on the debts of the deceased to avoid having to sell the property received from the will, to eliminate a costly court fight with the creditor, or as a matter of family honor.*

As in all other problems with an estate, the family may wish to consult with an attorney in this instance.

ESTATE AND INHERITANCE TAXES

Unlike some states, Illinois does not have estate or inheritance taxes in most cases. The only time estate taxes would be paid to the state of Illinois would be if the estate was subject to federal estate taxes and a credit was allowed for state taxes. Then these taxes would be paid to the state and credited against the federal tax due.

There is a federal estate tax for estates above a certain amount. Estates below that amount are allowed a *unified credit*, which exempts them from tax. The unified credit applies to the estate a person can leave at death and to gifts during his or her lifetime.

In May, 2001, the federal estate tax was changed again with the passage of The Economic Growth and Tax Relief Reconciliation Act of 2001. This act will increase available exemptions over time, gradually drop rates, and will repeal the federal estate tax in 2010. That is if this act is not amended again, which it very well may be especially for those years after 2010.

The key years for exemptions are:

Year	Amount
2001	$1 million
2004	$1.5 million
2006	$2 million
2009	$3.5 million

Basically this means that the above amounts can pass in a will without a federal estate tax charge. While these numbers look large, this is the total of all the assets of an estate including the home, land, stocks, etc. With an increasing real estate market and the value of other securities hopefully increasing, it is not beyond reason that a person who has lived a long life and invested wisely could have an estate valued over these amounts.

ANNUAL EXCLUSION

When a person makes a gift, that gift is subtracted from the amount entitled to the unified credit available to his or her estate at death. However, a person is allowed to make gifts of up to $10,000 per person per year without having these subtracted from the unified credit. This means a married couple can make gifts of up to $20,000 per year. The Taxpayer Relief Act of 1997 provided that this exclusion amount will be adjusted for inflation.

Deciding if You Need an Illinois Will

3

Illinois does not impose many requirements on those who wish to make a will. Any person who is eighteen years of age, of sound mind, and a resident of Illinois can make their own will. The phrase *of sound mind* means that a person is able to understand who his or her beneficiaries are and is able to direct his or her estate to these beneficiaries or others. Illinois courts have ruled that those who suffer from dementia or other mental disabilities can only create a valid will during those times when that person is lucid. This should be certified by a written statement from their physician, which is attached to the will.

What a Will Can Do

The intent of writing a will is to have control over the distribution of your estate after you have died. It should be written using clear language so that it is not confusing to those who are left to deal with the estate. A will is not a place to vent anger or disappointment with children, spouses, or other heirs. Personal messages such as this should be restricted to separate writings that will be distributed upon your death.

A will that uses vague confusing terms, does not follow Illinois laws, or uses precious space on personal messages has a greater chance of being declared invalid by a court.

BENEFICIARIES   A will allows you to decide who gets your property after your death. You can give specific personal items to certain persons and decide which of your friends or relatives, if any, deserve a greater share of your estate. You can leave gifts to schools and charities.

EXECUTOR   A will allows you to decide who will be the executor of your estate. An *executor* is the person who gathers together all your assets and distributes them to the beneficiaries, hires attorneys or accountants if necessary, and files any essential tax or probate forms. With a will, you can provide that your executor does not have to post a *surety bond* with the court in order to serve and this can save your estate some money. (A surety bond is a type of insurance policy that will pay for losses of an executor. An executor would obtain this from an insurance company who would first investigate the executor and then issue the policy for a dollar amount. Some surety bonds can be expensive, but it does protect the estate.)

You can also give the executor the power to sell your property and take other actions without getting a court order. An executor is sometimes referred to as a *personal representative.*

GUARDIAN   A will allows you to choose a guardian for your minor children. This way you can avoid fights among relatives and make sure the best person raises your children. You may also appoint separate guardians over your children and over their money. For example you may appoint your sister as guardian over your children, and your father as guardian over their money. That way, a second person can keep an eye on how the children's money is being spent.

PROTECTING HEIRS   You can set up a trust to provide that your property is not distributed immediately. Many people feel that their children would not be ready to handle large sums of money at the age of majority, which in Illinois is eighteen. A will can direct that the money is held until the children are twenty-one, twenty-five, or older.

MINIMIZING TAXES   If your estate is over $1,000,000 then it will be subject to federal estate taxes. (see Chapter 2.) If you wish to lower those taxes, for example by making gifts to charities, you can do so through a will. However, such estate planning is beyond the scope of this book and you should consult an estate planning attorney or another book for further information.

IF YOU HAVE NO WILL

If you do not have a will, the intestacy laws of the state determine who gets your property. As explained in Chapter 2, any property owned in joint tenancy would automatically go the joint owner, and any property held in trust would go to the beneficiaries. For non-trust property in your name alone, Illinois law says that your property shall be distributed as follows:

- If you leave a spouse and no children, your spouse gets your entire estate.

- If you leave a spouse and children, your spouse gets half of your estate and the children get equal shares of the remainder.

- If you leave no spouse, all of your children get equal shares of your estate.

- If you leave no spouse and no children, then your estate would go to the highest persons on the following list who are living:
  - your parents;
  - your brothers and sisters, or if dead, their children;
  - your grandparents;
  - your uncles and aunts or their descendants;
  - your great-grandparents or their descendants; and
  - the state of Illinois.

Additionally without a will the probate court will appoint a guardian for your children and for their inheritance; and an executor to collect your assets and settle your estate.

OUT-OF-STATE WILLS

A will that is valid in another state would probably be valid to pass property in Illinois. However, if the will is not *self-proved*, before it could be accepted by an Illinois probate court a person in your former state would have to be appointed as a *commissioner* to take the oath of a person who witnessed your signature on the will. Because of the expense and delay in having a commissioner appointed and the problems in finding out-of-state witnesses, it is advisable to execute a new will after moving to Illinois.

The problem with wills that are created and are valid in other states stem from each state having different laws that govern wills. Even if the laws are identical, any out of state document is looked at differently by attorneys and judges. One of the goals of writing a will is to make the distribution of your estate as easy as possible on your heirs. By relying on an out of state will you take the chance that someone who thinks they should be getting a bigger cut of the estate will be able to convince a court that the out of state will is not valid.

Illinois also allows a will to be *self-proved* so that the witnesses never have to be called in to take an oath. With special self-proving language in your will the witnesses take the oath at the time of signing and never have to be seen again.

A self-proved clause is added at the end of a will, after the place where the make of the will and the witnesses sign their name. It contains a place for the seal and signature of a notary public. The notary signs and verifies under oath that the maker of the will and the witnesses are the people they say that they are and that they did actually sign this will. A *notary public* is commonly used in legal documents to verify that the person did sign the document.

NOTE: *Illinois, unlike many other states, does NOT require a self-proved clause. Its purpose is to verify that the signatures are authentic. This can be important if, after the maker of the will and all witnesses have died, the court finds some irregularity in the signing of the will. For this reason, a* SELF-PROVED AFFIDAVIT *is added as a separate page to each will in this book.*

WHAT A WILL CANNOT DO

A will cannot direct that anything illegal be done and it cannot put unreasonable conditions on a gift. A provision that your daughter gets all of your property if she divorces her husband would be ignored by the court. She would get the property with no conditions attached. To be sure that conditions listed in your will are enforceable you should consult with an attorney.

A will cannot leave money or property to an animal because animals cannot legally own property. If you wish to continue paying for care of an animal after your death, you should leave the funds in trust or to a friend whom you know will care for the animal. (See Chapter 12 on trusts.)

CONDITIONS   If you wish to put some sort of conditions or restrictions on the property you leave, you should consult a lawyer. For example, if you want to leave money to your brother only if he quits smoking, or to a hospital only if they name a wing in your honor, you should consult an attorney to be sure that these conditions are valid in your state.

USING A SIMPLE WILL

The wills in this book will pass your property whether your estate is $1,000 or $100,000,000. However, if your estate is over $625,000 (this amount will rise to $1,000,000 by 2006) then you might be able to avoid estate taxes by using a trust or other tax-saving device. The larger your estate, the more you can save on estate taxes by doing more complicated planning. If you have a large estate, or believe that your future assets will grow into a large estate, and are concerned about estate taxes you should consult an estate planning attorney.

WHO SHOULD NOT USE A SIMPLE WILL

WILL CONTEST

If you expect that there may be a fight over your estate or that some-one might contest your will's validity, you should consult a lawyer. If you leave less than the statutory share of your estate to your spouse or if you leave one or more of your children out of your will, it is likely that someone will contest your will.

Do not underestimate the potential for one of your heirs to initiate a will contest. A will contest can happen in the best of families, to people who for years got along with each other. Some people, when faced with the possibility of receiving property or money for free, will go to any lengths. There is also the possibility of your heirs being influenced by others into starting a will contest.

COMPLICATED ESTATES

If you are, or will be, the beneficiary of a trust or have any complications in your legal relationships, you may need special provisions in your will.

BLIND OR UNABLE TO WRITE

A person who is blind or who can sign only an "X" should also consult a lawyer about the proper way to make and execute a will.

ESTATES OVER $1 MILLION

If you expect to have an estate valued over $1,000,000 at the time of your death, you may want to consult with a CPA or tax attorney regarding tax consequences.

Even though $1,000,000 may seem like a large amount now, remember this includes all the property in your estate; cash, stocks, personal property, and real property. If your estate includes items that normally increase in value over time, (for example; stocks, bonds, artwork, coin collections, fine jewelry, land, etc.) your estate may exceed the $1,000,000 value by the time of your death. (see Chapter 2.)

UNDERSTANDING PROBATE 4

There are many misconceptions about probate court. This court is not just reserved for the wealthy, nor are all actions of this court negative toward the heirs of an estate. A probate court will do all in its power to handle the estate in accordance with the terms of the will, which is why it is so important to have a will.

According to Illinois law the person who holds the will must file the will in probate court within 30 days of the death of the will's maker. The primary reason for the probate court is to oversee the distribution of assets in accordance with the will. This court intervention protects the heirs from unscrupulous people who prey on the grieving and make sure that the terms of the will are carried out. The court will also supervise any investments or sale of property to make sure that the executor acts in the best interest of all the heirs.

Another protection from the probate court is that guardians who are named by the will are then accountable to the court for their actions. If the appointed guardian of a minor is unable to perform the duties of a guardian, the court will step in to protect that minor.

The court also makes sure that all potential heirs have been notified and will handle any challenges to the distribution of assets. Sometimes, after the will is filed with the probate court and all potential heirs have been notified, those who rightly or wrongly believe that they should benefit from the will may file a claim or challenge with the court. The probate court's experience allows these claims to be efficiently and honestly resolved. This may be why many of those who wish to attempt a fraud by claiming to be a beneficiary will stop their claim once the court is involved. Just the idea of hiring a probate attorney and appearing in front of a judge may deter those with frivolous claims from making such a challenge.

If the deceased was involved in a legal action, such as a personal injury suit, or if the heirs are bringing a wrongful death suit, other courts may require that an estate be opened in probate court. This is done to guarantee that any monetary results, such as a settlement or an award from these suits, are distributed according to the provisions of the will. Some insurance companies may also require that an estate be opened prior to dispensing the proceeds of an insurance contract.

OPENING AN ESTATE

In probate court the act of filing a will with the court is called the *Opening of an Estate*. The estate is opened with the circuit court in the county where the deceased resided. Each county has its own requirements for forms that must be used in opening an estate. For information on opening an estate call the circuit court of the county where the estate is to be filed, they can direct you to the proper forms and may be able to provide assistance as to the other requirements.

When a will is filed in the probate court a judge determines if the will is valid. If the judge determines that the will is valid, assets will be distributed according to the terms of the will. If the will is found invalid the assets will be distributed in accordance with state laws (as if there were no will).

Please note that just because a will is filed with the court and the estate is opened does not necessarily mean that the will must be probated. Small estates, wills that are filed due to some insurance company requirements or for other ancillary reasons may not have to be probated.

Probate is actually the legal procedure for the orderly distribution of property in a person's estate under court supervision.

PERSONAL REPRESENTATIVE

A personal representative is the person or office who manages the decedent's estate. An executor or administrator is a type of personal representative. Depending on the size an complexity of the estate, a person, a bank, a trust company, a law office, or combination of these may by appointed as personal representatives in accordance with the terms of the will.

DUTIES Duties of a personal representative are defined by the Illinois Probate Act and the Internal Revenue Code. The executor or personal representative has the legal duty to act in the interests of the deceased, following the wishes that were expressed in the will.

Although counties vary, duties generally consist of:

- publish required legal notice;

- keep records of all transactions of the estate;

- pay final bills of the deceased;

- notify insurance, trust and stock companies of death;

- collect and prepare an inventory list of all property;

- secure appropriate valuations and appraisals of assets;

- preserve, manage and insure estate assets;

- approve or contest claims against the estate;

- file accountings showing distribution of assets and increases in assets;

- provide beneficiaries with appropriate tax information; and

- file all necessary tax returns for the estate.

When a will is probated the probate court will oversee that these duties are fulfilled in accordance with the terms of the will. For complex estates the personal representative or executor may require the assistance of an attorney who is experienced with probate law. As with the executor, the estate pays the fees of attorneys and other professional services to the estate.

Since the serious duties of an executor can be a lot of work, it is important that the person selected as executor agree to take on this task. For this reason, you may wish to discuss the duties with the person prior to naming them as your executor.

Making a
Simple Will 5

A simple will is one that has a limited amount of clauses and can be written in just a few pages. This book provides samples of simple wills in Appendix A. You may want to refer back to these samples while reading this chapter.

Parties in Your Will

Parties to a will include all those who are mentioned in the will and who receive your estate upon your death. Make sure that you identify these parties by their correct name. You should also review whom the State of Illinois considers your beneficiaries; this is discussed in Chapter 3 under the section "If You Have No Will".

PEOPLE   When making your will, it is important to correctly identify the persons you name in your will. In some families, names differ only by middle initial or by Jr. or Sr. Be sure to check the names before you make your will. You can also add your relationship to the party, and their location such as *"my cousin, Michael Kane of Springfield, Illinois."*

ORGANIZATIONS   The same applies to organizations and charities.

Example: There is more than one group using the words "cancer society" or "heart association" in their names. Be sure to get the correct name of the group you intend to leave your gift.

SPOUSE AND
CHILDREN

In most states, you must mention your spouse and children in your will even if you do not leave them property. That is to show that you are of sound mind and know who are your legal heirs. As mentioned earlier, if you have a spouse and/or children and plan to leave your property to persons other than them, you should consult an attorney to be sure that your will is enforceable.

SPECIFIC BEQUESTS

You may wish to give certain items of personal property or a particular dollar amount to specific people, organizations, or to charities after your death. Some states allow a will to reference a list of these specific gifts, which can be updated periodically. In Illinois, if you wish to incorporate such a list into your will that list must be complete at the time you sign your will and then can only be changed by CODICIL TO WILL. (see form 17, p.157.) For this reason, specific bequests of personal property or cash are listed within the will itself.

In the simple will forms in Appendix B, there is a section provided ("Second") for listing these gifts. If you do not wish to use this section, merely cross it out. Giving specific gifts is not required to make a will legal. However, many people want to choose who gets certain items such a family heirlooms or wish to honor a particular charity after they die.

GIVING SPECIFIC
ITEMS

There are some things to remember in giving specific bequests in a will. By the time of your death; (1) you may not own the specific item or (2) the property may have declined in value.

Example: The gift "my mother's silver brooch to my cousin Judith Smith," could be a problem if, at the time of a person's death, mother's brooch had been sold. In that case Judith Smith would get nothing.

One approach to solve this is to put a dollar value on the item you wish to give. So the above gift could be worded "my mother's silver brooch or $250." Another approach is to group items; "all of my jewelry," "all of the books in my collection," "my entire doll collection," "all of my mother's jewelry." That way your beneficiary would still get something, assuming that there was still one item left in a category.

Example: Joe wanted his two children to equally share his estate. His will left his son his stocks (worth $500,000 at the time) and his daughter $500,000 in cash. By the time of Joe's death the stock was only worth $100,000. The son would get the $100,000 stock and the daughter would receive $500,000 in cash, provided that Joe's estate had $500,000 in cash.

In this example the property has declined in value since the will was written. In order to have Joe's wishes, that each of his children get an equal share of his estate, honored. He should have left 50% of his estate to each child. Using percentages would allow the estate to be divided fairly.

JOINT BENEFICIARIES

Be careful about leaving one item of personal property to more than one person. For example, if you leave something to your son and his wife, what would happen if they divorce? Even if you leave something to two of your own children, what if they can't agree about who will have possession of it? Whenever possible, leave property to one person.

LOCATION OF SPECIFIC BEQUESTS IN A WILL

Again, your will need not contain a section for giving specific bequests. However, if it is an important part of your estate plan, you can give certain items or particular dollar amounts to named people, organizations or charities, but remember to make changes in your will by CODICIL TO WILL as your assets change. (see form 17, p.157.) In Illinois, the section for listing these specific gifts is at the beginning of a will. (See "Second" in the wills in Appendix B of this book).

The placement at the beginning of a will is to ensure that the specific bequests have priority. Which means that the gifts will be distributed out of the estate before the rest of the will is honored.

Example: Mary Jones leaves a will stating that; 1) The first Congregational Church in Joliet receives $500, and 2) the rest of her estate goes to her niece, Heather.

If at the time of her death Mary Jones' estate is worth $1,200 then the church will get the $500 and her niece will receive $700. However, if at the time of her death Mary Jones' estate is worth $400, then the church will receive the $400 and her niece will receive nothing.

REMAINDER CLAUSE

After the section on specific gifts, the next section of an Illinois will should give the *remainder* of a person's estate. (See "Third" in the wills in Appendix B of this book.) The *remainder clause* is one of the most important parts of the will. This is the clause that says something like "all the rest of my property, I leave to…" This clause makes sure that the will disposes of all property owned at the time of death and that nothing is forgotten.

If a will only gives specific gifts and there is no remainder clause, the remainder of a person's estate will pass as if there was no will. In using the forms in Appendix B of this book, make sure to complete the "Third" section, which is the remainder clause.

ALTERNATE BENEFICIARIES

You should always provide for an *alternate beneficiary* in case the first one dies before you do and you do not have a chance to make out a new will.

SURVIVOR OR DESCENDANTS

Suppose your will leaves your property to your sister and brother, but your brother predeceases you. Should his share go to your sister or to your brother's children or grandchildren?

If you are giving property to two or more persons and if you want it all to go to the other if one of them dies, then you would specify "or the survivor of them."

If, on the other hand, you want the property to go to the children of the deceased person you should state in your will, "or their lineal descendants" of the person. This would include his or her children and grandchildren.

FAMILY OR PERSON

If you decide you want it to go to your brother's children, you must next decide if an equal share should go to each family or to each person.

Example: Suppose your brother leaves three grandchildren, and one is an only child of his daughter and the others are the children of his son. If you want all the grandchildren get an equal share of your estate, then you would specify *per capita*. On the other hand, if the grandchildren should take their parent's share, it is *per stirpes*.

In naming lineal descendants you must decide whether the property shall pass per stirpes or per capita. *Per stirpes* means that each branch of the family gets an equal share. *Per capita* means that each person gets an equal share. Illinois law assumes per stirpes unless otherwise stated in the will. The wills in this book use per stirpes.

Example: Alice leaves her property to her two daughters, Mary and Pat in equal shares, or to their lineal descendants per stirpes. Both daughters die before Alice. Mary leaves one child, Pat leaves two children. In this case Mary's child would get half of the estate and Pat's children would split the other half of the estate. If Alice had specified per capita instead of per stirpes then each child would have gotten one-third of the estate.

Per Stirpes Distribution

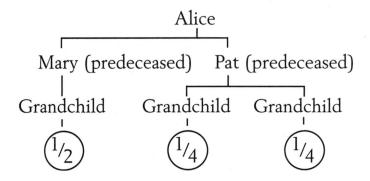

Per Capita Distribution

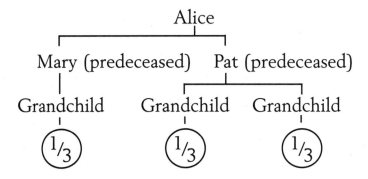

There are fourteen different wills in this book, but you may want to divide your property slightly differently from what is stated in these wills. If so you can re-type the wills according to these rules, specifying whether the property should go to the survivor or the lineal descendants. If this is confusing to you, you should consider seeking the advice of an attorney.

SURVIVORSHIP

Many people put a clause in their will stating that anyone receiving property under the will must survive for thirty days (or forty-five or sixty) after the death of the person who made the will. This is so that if the two people die in the same accident, there will not be two probates and the property will not go to the other party's heirs.

Example: Fred and Wilma were married and each had children by previous marriages. They did not have survivorship clauses in their wills and they died in an airplane crash. Fred's children hired several expert witnesses and a large law firm to prove that at the time of the crash Fred lived for a few minutes longer than Wilma. That way, when Wilma died first, all of her property went to Fred. When he died a few minutes later, all of Fred *and* Wilma's property went to his children. Wilma's children got nothing.

GUARDIANSHIP

If you have minor children you should name a guardian for them. There are two types of guardians—a guardian over the *person* and a guardian over the *property*. The first is the person who decides where the children will live and makes the other parental decisions for them. A guardian of the property is in charge of the minor's property and inheritance. In most cases, one person is appointed guardian of both the person and property. But some people prefer the children to live with one person, but to have the money held by another person.

Example: Sandra was a widow with a young daughter. She knew that if anything happened to her, her sister would be the best person to raise her daughter. But her sister was never good with money. So, when Sandra made out her will, she named her sister as guardian over the person of her daughter and she named her father as guardian over the estate of her daughter.

If you have dependents such with a disability or elderly you may also wish to appoint a guardian to oversee any inheritance that they will receive. The guardianship of these dependents and even your pets may be better served through setting up a trust. This type of trust would be able to limit the powers of the guardian or trustee, detail the investments and expenditures, and provide for life-time care. You should contact an estate planning attorney who has experience in trusts to set this type of trust up for you.

When naming a guardian, it is always advisable to name an alternate guardian in case your first choice is unable to serve for any reason.

CHILDREN'S TRUST

When a parent dies leaving a minor child and the child's property is held by a guardian, the guardianship ends when the child reaches the age of eighteen, and all the property is turned over to the child. Many parents do not feel their children are competent at the age of eighteen to handle large sums of money and prefer that it be held until the child is twenty-one or older.

If you wish to set up a complicated system of determining when your children should receive various amounts of your estate, if you have a special needs child that will require life-long support after your death, or if you want the property held to a higher age than eighteen, then you should consult a lawyer to draft a trust. However, if you want a simple provision that the funds be held until your children reach eighteen, and you have someone you trust to make decisions about paying for education or other expenses for your child or children, you can put that provision in your will as a children's' trust.

The children's' trust trustee can be the same person as the guardian or a different person. It is advisable to name an alternate trustee if your first choice is unable to handle the job when the time comes. (See Chapter 12 on trusts.)

EXECUTORS

An *executor* (also called *personal representative* or *administrator*) is the person who is responsible for settling a deceased person's estate. An executor can be any U.S. citizen over the age of 18 who has not been convicted of a felony. He or she will gather your assets, handle the sale of them if necessary, prepare an inventory, hire an attorney, and distribute the property.

An executor should be a person you trust. You can state in your will that no *bond* will be required to be posted by him or her, otherwise the court will require that a surety bond be paid for by your estate to guaranty that the executor is honest.

It is best to appoint an Illinois resident as an executor, both because it is easier and because a bond may be required of a non-resident even if your will waives it.

Some people like to name two persons as executor to avoid jealousy, or to have them check on each other's honesty. However, this is not a good idea. It makes double work in getting the papers signed, and there can be problems if they cannot agree on something. You can, however, name an alternate executor to take over if the first executor is unable to fulfill the job or has died.

Per Illinois law, the executor of your estate is entitled to reasonable compensation for his or her time and effort used in handling your estate. To guarantee that your executor receives a fee for his or her work, you may wish to include a clause like "…It is my wish that my executor be paid the appropriate executor's fees for his/her services," after the sentence where you name your executor.

If you trust your executor you can also include a clause that gives your executor *full power and authority* to sell your real property and personal possessions. On the other hand, if you wish to specifically limit your executor's powers you can include a list of these limitations in your will. Because the issue of executor's powers is complex you may wish to consider seeking the advice of an attorney.

WITNESSES

Signing your will must be witnessed by two persons to be valid in Illinois. In some states three witnesses are required, so if you own property in other states, you may need to have three witnesses to your will. In some states a will that is entirely handwritten, called a *holographic will*, is valid without witnesses. In Illinois *any* will is *invalid* without two credible, disinterested witnesses.

Credible witnesses are those who understand what you are signing. This would eliminate a 3-year-old, someone who is mentally incompetent, or the family pet. While Illinois does not require witnesses to be over 18 years old, it is best if all witnesses are 18 or over. A *disinterested* witness is someone who is NOT mentioned in the will or is not receiving anything from the estate.

Under Illinois law, people who are beneficiaries to your will *cannot* also be a witness to your will. Not only are the witnesses prohibited from benefitting from a will that they witness; the witnesses spouses and decedents (children) also cannot benefit from that will.

SELF-PROVING AFFIDAVIT

A will needs two witnesses to be legal, and if you also include a notarized SELF-PROVED WILL AFFIDAVIT, the will may be admitted to probate much faster. The SELF-PROVED WILL AFFIDAVIT is a separate sheet of paper that is attached to your will. (It is the last page of each will in Appendix B.) It includes the signatures of both you and your witnesses; these signatures are then notarized on this form. The signing and notarization is usually done at the same time that your will is signed and witnessed.

A will is valid without a SELF-PROVED WILL AFFIDAVIT. However, the probating of a will without this document may be delayed while the court verifies the validity of the witnesses signatures and the procedure used to sign the will.

DISINHERITING SOMEONE

Because it may result in your will being challenged in court, you should not make your own will if you intend to disinherit someone. However, you may wish to leave one child less than another because you already made a gift to that child, or perhaps that child needs the money less than the other.

If you do give more to one child than to another, then you should state your reasons to show that you thought out your plan. Otherwise the one who receives less might argue that you did not realize what you were doing and were not competent to make a will. If a person is judged 'not competent' to make a will, his or her entire will can be ignored by order of the court.

FUNERAL ARRANGEMENTS

There is no harm in stating your preferences in your will, but directions for a funeral are not legally enforceable and many times a will is not found until after the funeral. Therefore it is better to tell your family about your wishes or to make prior arrangements yourself.

You may wish to arrange and prepay for your own funeral as a part of your long-range estate planning and to be guaranteed that your funeral will completely reflect your wishes. Again, notify your immediate family if you make these arrangements.

FORMS

There are several different forms included in this book for easy use. You can tear them out, photocopy them, or you can retype them on plain paper.

CAUTIONS

HANDWRITTEN
WILLS

In some states a person can write out a will by hand, and even without witnesses it is valid. This is called a *holographic will,* but in Illinois such a will is not valid.

CORRECTIONS

Your will can be typed or handwritten or a filled-in form. It should have no white-outs or erasures. If for some reason it is impossible to make a will without corrections, they should be initialed by you and both witnesses. However, it is better to re-copy the will without any corrections to avoid the potential of will contests after your death.

MULTIPLE PAGES

If there are two or more pages they should be fastened together, each page should be initialed by you and by the witnesses, and each page numbered.

Example: A three-page will would be page numbered; 1 of 3, 2 of 3, 3 of 3.

EXECUTING YOUR WILL 6

In the state of Illinois, the signing of a will is a serious legal event and must be done properly or the will may be declared invalid. Preferably it should be done in a private area without distraction. All parties must watch each other sign and no one should leave the room until all have signed.

Example: Ebenezer was bedridden in a small room. When he signed his will the witnesses could not actually see his hand because the dresser was in the way. His will was ignored by the court and his property went to persons not named in the will.

PROCEDURE

To be sure your will is valid, you should follow some rules.

- Make a statement to your witness, such as: "This is my will. I have read it and I understand it and this is how I want it to read. I want you two people to witness me signing my will and sign your names as witnesses."

- You do not have to read your will to the witnesses nor do you have to let them read it. Legally, the witnesses are only witnessing your above statement about this document being your will and the your signing of your name to the document.

- You must date your will and sign your name at the end of the document in ink exactly as it is printed in the will.

- You should also initial each page if your will has more than one page.

- The witnesses must watch your actual signing and initialing of your will.

- The witness must sign their names at the end of the will and initial each page in ink.

- You and the witness must watch as each witness signs their name and initials each page.

Self-Proving Affidavit

As explained in the last chapter, it is a good idea to attach a Self-Proved Will Affidavit to your will. This means that you will need to have a *notary public* present to watch everyone sign. If it is impossible to have a notary public present, your will is still valid, but the probate procedure may be delayed.

After your witnesses have signed as attesting witnesses under your name, you and they should sign the self-proving page and the notary should notarize it. (The notary cannot be one of your witnesses.)

It is a good idea to make at lease one copy of your will, but you should not personally sign the copies or have them notarized. The reason for this is if you cancel or intentionally destroy your will to revoke it, upon your death someone may produce a copy and have it probated.

AFTER SIGNING YOUR WILL 7

A will is a legal document. Because it is not filed in any court when it is written, if the will is lost or stolen there is no record that the will ever existed. A will is also a private document, which can cause hurt feelings in a family if the terms of the will are released early. Therefore the safety and security of a will is very important. To complicate the issue, this document must be able to be found after the person who knows the most about it (the person who made the will) is gone.

STORING YOUR WILL

Your will should be kept in a place safe from fire and easily accessible to your heirs. Your executor should know of its whereabouts. It can be kept in a home safe or fire box or in a safe deposit box in a bank. In some states a will should not be placed in a safe deposit box because they are sealed at death, but in Illinois, it is easy to get a will and burial documents out of a deceased person's safe deposit box.

Wills are not filed anywhere until after a person's death. No one has to know what you have put in your will while you are alive. If you name a trust company or bank as an executor, it will hold your will in safe-keeping. Often an attorney preparing a will might offer to keep it in his safe deposit box at no charge. This way he or she will likely be contacted at the time of death and will be in a good position to do the lucrative probate work. However, many Illinois lawyers are now discontinuing this service.

REVOKING YOUR WILL

The usual way to revoke a will is to execute a new will, which states that it revokes all previously made wills. To revoke a will without making a new will, one can tear, burn, deface, obliterate, or destroy the will; or one can direct someone else to do the same in his or her presence. As long as these acts are done with the intention of revoking the will, then it is legally revoked. If this is done accidentally or as a criminal act to manipulate the results of probate, then the will is not legally revoked.

Example: Ralph tells his son Clyde to go to the basement safe and tear up Ralph's will. If Clyde does not tear it up in Ralph's presence it is probably not effectively revoked.

REVIVAL What if you change your will by drafting a new one and later decide you do not like the changes and want to go back to your old will? Can you destroy the new will and revive the old one? *No!* Once you execute a new will revoking the old will, you cannot revive the old will unless you execute a new document stating that you intend to revive the old will. In other words, you should execute a new will.

UPDATING YOUR WILL

You should not make any changes to your will after it has been signed. If you cross out a person's name or add a clause to a will that has already been signed, the change you make will not be valid and your entire will might be declared invalid by the probate court.

In Illinois, the only way to change a signed will is to execute a document called a CODICIL TO WILL. (see form 17, p.157.) A CODICIL TO WILL is an amendment to a will and it must be executed just like a will, using the exact procedures as listed in Chapter 6. There must be two witnesses to the CODICIL TO WILL and it should have a self-proving affidavit that is notarized.

A person may make an unlimited number of codicils to a will, but each one must be executed with the same formality as a full will. Because a CODICIL TO WILL requires this same formality, it is sometimes easier just to create a new will.

MAKING AN ADVANCE DIRECTIVE: THE LIVING WILL

8

Advance Directive is the general term that refers to your oral and written instructions about your future medical care, in the event that you become unable to speak for yourself. This general term is often used in hospitals or by other professionals. In Illinois there are two legal types of written Advance Directives, the *living will* and the *health care power of attorney*. (see Chapters 8 and 9.)

No, a *living will* is not a video tape of a person making a will. It has nothing to do with the usual type of will that distributes property. A LIVING WILL DECLARATION is a document by which a person declares that he or she does not want artificial life support systems used if he or she becomes terminally ill. (see form 18, p.159.) A LIVING WILL DECLARATION also provides that a person receive only that care necessary to maintain comfort and dignity, while death is permitted to take its natural course.

In 1984, Illinois passed a law which allowed anyone who is of sound mind and over the age of eighteen to create their own LIVING WILL DECLARATION. Reasons for having a living will are to ensure that a person's wishes about their death will be honored and to protect family, friends, and health care professionals from making critical decisions about a dying person without knowing what that person would want. Under Illinois law, a living will has no effect on the health care of a person until that person has been certified in writing to be terminally ill by a physician.

The LIVING WILL DECLARATION prohibits doctors from using "death delaying procedures" on the terminally ill patient. These procedures specifically include such things as:

- assisted ventilation;

- artificial kidney treatments;

- intravenous treatments;

- blood transfusions; and,

- other procedures that serve only to delay certain death.

However, the Illinois Living Wills Act will not allow nutrition or hydration to be withheld or withdrawn if death would result solely from dehydration or starvation. In addition, the use of medication to relieve pain or to comfort the patient is not affected by a living will. The Illinois law calls the person who makes a living will a *declarant* and the living will itself a *declaration*.

Under the Illinois law, a LIVING WILL DECLARATION must be signed in front of two witnesses, who also sign the document. The witnesses must be at least eighteen years old, and not financially responsible for the health care of the declarant (the person creating their living will). Witnesses cannot be a beneficiary through a will or able to inherit from the declarant. Also, witnesses cannot sign for the declarant. If the person is physically unable to sign their own LIVING WILL DECLARATION, they may read their LIVING WILL DECLARATION out loud and direct another person to sign it for them.

After you have created your living will, provide your attending physician with a copy. In many Illinois hospitals, you will be asked to provide the hospital with a copy of your living will when you are being admitted. Living wills can be revoked in the same manner as all other wills; tearing, burning, obliterating, or by written revocation. Under Illinois law, health care providers are protected from civil and criminal liability for complying with living wills. Physicians generally honor a patient's LIVING WILL DECLARATION to the best of their abilities.

A LIVING WILL DECLARATION form is included in Appendix B of this book. (see form 18, p.159.) This form is the same one included in the actual Illinois law. Although this form may look complex at first, it is always better to use forms which are part of the law and are a familiar format for health care professionals. While a living will does not have to be on that form to be legal, many health care professionals are not comfortable with another format, so it is best to use the statutory form rather than make up your own.

Making an Advance Directive: The Health Care Power of Attorney

9

A health care power of attorney or medical power of attorney is another type of advance directive. As with a living will, this is used when you are unable to make decisions about your medical care. With a health care power of attorney you do not have to be terminally ill, as with a living will, merely unable to express your own healthcare desires.

There are several types of powers of attorney for such matters as health care, finances, real estate, and child care. (see Chapter 10 for information on property power of attorney.)

Health Care Power of Attorney

A Living Will Declaration comes into effect only when a person is certified to be terminally ill, however a Power of Attorney for Health Care can come into effect in a non-terminal condition, such as an irreversible coma. (see form 19, p.161.) This document is designed to give you the most control of your health care at a point when you are unable to communicate your desires. With this document you (1) appoint someone (your *agent*) to speak for you in matters of health care and (2) provide detailed instructions on how this agent is to act. For example: you can instruct your agent when to withhold food or fluids, when to order CPR (cardiopulmonary resuscitation) be stopped, or what specific types of treatment should be administered.

Anyone over the age of eighteen (called the *principal*) can draw up a POWER OF ATTORNEY FOR HEALTH CARE. The person you select as your agent must be at least eighteen years old, and cannot be your doctor or someone who is paid to provide you with health care services. Before selecting someone to act as your agent, discuss this with them to determine if they can act according to your wishes. You may also appoint successor agents in case the primary agent is unavailable or unable to act.

You may specify when the POWER OF ATTORNEY FOR HEALTH CARE begins and ends. If there is no termination date, the document will continue until your death.

A POWER OF ATTORNEY FOR HEALTH CARE should be signed in front of a witness, who also signs the document. The witness should not be the person appointed as your agent or as a successor agent. You may also have your agent and successor agents sign the document, but this is not required by law.

Most other state laws recognize a POWER OF ATTORNEY FOR HEALTH CARE, with some variations. It is suggested that you consult an attorney if you will be residing in another state.

An Illinois POWER OF ATTORNEY FOR HEALTH CARE is in Appendix B of this book. (see form 19, p.161.) This form is the same one included in the Illinois Law. The form looks confusing and long, that is because the instructions for filling out the form are printed within the form. A POWER OF ATTORNEY FOR HEALTH CARE does not have to be on this form to be legal. A shorter version can be used as long as it expresses the same intentions as listed in form 19. However, it is always better to use the forms which are part of the actual law. As with any legal document, you may wish to have an attorney review this document.

You should talk to your doctor about advance directives. Your doctor may be able to better explain situations in which the person appointed in your health care power of attorney may be required to act. After you have signed a living will and/or a health care power of attorney, provide a copy to your doctor. You should consider signing both a living will and a health care power of attorney to cover any future medical condition.

IF YOU DO NOTHING

If you do not have a living will or a health care power of attorney, the Health Care Surrogate Act may allow certain persons to make medical and life sustaining healthcare decisions in your behalf when you are unable to speak for yourself. A court may be asked to appoint a special guardian to make these decisions or a physician may rely on the following surrogates as listed in the Health Care Surrogate Act:

- the patient's guardian;

- the patient's spouse;

- the patient's adult children;

- the patient's parents;

- the patient's brothers or sisters;

- the patient's grandchildren; or,

- a close friend of the patient.

In cases were there are several people in the above categories, those surrogates will be forced to decide among themselves on the healthcare decisions.

The most compelling reason for a person to create an advance directive is to avoid the tremendous heartache, confusion, second-guessing, and guilt that a surrogate feels after making these types of decisions. No matter the age or the medical history of a loved one, having to make these types of life and death decisions without any guidance from the ill loved one is a cruel burden.

MAKING A PROPERTY POWER OF ATTORNEY

10

Many of us are familiar with what is called *durable power of attorney for property*. We use it in real estate transactions when we are unable to be in attendance at certain legal proceedings and other contract actions. This is a very powerful document which allows someone else to have total control over items of property, contracts, or even your name for a certain period of time or in a particular instance. Like the Health Care Power of Attorney (see Chapter 9), the Property Power of Attorney can be made part of your estate plan.

The power of attorney for property allows for a principal (the person making the power of attorney) to appoint an *agent* to handle matters of finance and property. The agent's powers can be limited to a particular transaction, to transactions regarding particular property, by date, by certain events, or by other limiting factors. Also, this type of power of attorney can be written so that the agent has complete power of all the property and business affairs of the principal. This is the primary reason why this type of document must be drafted with particular care.

What a property power of attorney usually covers:

- real estate transactions;

- financial institution transactions;

- stock and bond transactions;

- personal property transactions;

- safe deposit box transactions;

- insurance and annuity transactions;

- retirement plan transactions;

- social security, employment and military service benefits;

- tax matters;

- commodity and option transactions;

- business operations; and

- all other property powers and transactions.

You can list several agents and even successor agents in this power of attorney. You can specifically limit the agent's powers by particular instruction and by date. For an estate plan, you may wish to give an agent powers to run your business, maintain your investments, or act in your behalf with a financial institution if you become incapacitated and cannot speak for yourself; the powers to end when you recover.

> ***Warning***: This document can be used by the unscrupulous to obtain control of a person's property and complete financial matters. By simply neglecting to indicate a termination date, a principal can inadvertently give an agent continuous powers to make financial decisions even after the principal is able to make their own decisions. In some cases, the elderly sign away their property with this document, in the mistaken belief that they are about to die, only to recover and find out that they no longer have any control of their property.

NOTE: *Because this document must be drafted with such care, there is no form in this book for a property power of attorney. You are urged to get the assistance of a professional before you sign such a document.*

MAKING ANATOMICAL GIFTS 11

Since 1969, Illinois has allowed its residents to donate their bodies or organs for research or transplantation. Consent may be given by a relative of a deceased person but, because relatives are often in shock or too upset to make such a decision, it is better to have one's intent made clear before death. This can be done by a statement in a will, by a signed document such as a **UNIFORM DONOR CARD**, or by properly executing the form on the reverse side of your Illinois driver's license. (see form 20, p.163.) The gift may be of all or part of one's body, and it may be made to a specific person such as a physician or an ill relative.

The document making the donation must be signed before two witnesses who must also sign in each other's presence. If the donor cannot sign, then the document may be signed for him at his direction in the presence of the witnesses. The donor may designate in the document who the physician is who will carry out the procedure.

After completing the proper document, the best thing you can do to ensure that your wishes to become a donor are honored is to tell your family. After your death, your family will be asked for permission to donate. If they know your wishes now, they will be prepared to honor your request.

If the document or will has been delivered to a specific donee, it may be amended or revoked by the donor in the following ways:

- by executing and delivering a signed statement to the donee;

- by an oral statement to two witnesses communicated to the donee;

- by an oral statement during a terminal illness made to an attending physician and communicated to the donee; or

- by a signed document found on the person of the donor or in his or her effects.

If a document of a gift has not been delivered to a donee it may be revoked by any of the above methods or by destruction, cancellation, or mutilation of the document. It may also be revoked in the same method a will is revoked as described in Chapter 7.

A UNIFORM DONOR CARD is included in Appendix B. (see form 20, p.163.) It must be signed in the presence of two signing witnesses.

UNDERSTANDING TRUSTS 12

After going through this book you may have decided that your estate is too complex or that you need certain things that a simple will just cannot provide. You may want to consider setting up a *trust* or several trusts as part of your estate plan. This book is not intended to help you draft a trust. That should be left to an experienced estate planning attorney who can incorporate a trust into your estate plan if you need one. This chapter is merely an overview on some uses for trusts and how they can be used in a comprehensive estate plan.

LAND TRUST

Illinois is one of the few states which allow real property (your home) to be put into a *land trust*. There are several reasons why you may want to do this. If you wish to keep the name of the actual owner of the property from public record, you could put the property in a land trust. Then the name of the trust would be listed as the owner of record.

Another reason to do this is that the beneficiary of a land trust will receive the property under the terms of the trust upon your death as if it were held in joint tenancy. This type of trust has lost much of its original power with the changes in tax laws, however it still may be useful in your estate plan.

Land trusts can be created so that they provide for the owners of the property and name the beneficiary.

Example: Bob Neil and his wife, Amy are elderly. They have one child, Steven, who lives in another state. Bob and Amy want Steven to get their home after both of them pass on. Bob and Amy set up a land trust with the bank that puts the property in the name of the trust, gives Bob and Amy a lifetime right to live in and sell their home, and names Steven as beneficiary. For an annual fee, the bank maintains the trust. After both Bob and Amy die, Steven is given the deed to the home.

LIVING TRUST

A *revocable trust* is usually the centerpiece of any estate plan. This document will bring together your assets in one private document. This document can be changed at any time during your lifetime without the need to make a codicil as in a will. You will probably want to place your home and your other assets under this trust. Your estate planning attorney can assist you with this.

You may also wish to create trusts for your children, any incapacitated dependants, or even your pets. A trust can be set up that will provide a certain level of funds to these people after your death. In setting up these trusts, you may be able to save certain taxes by funding the trusts with monetary gifts. For these types of trusts you should select a competent trustee who will maintain the trusts after you die.

OTHER TRUSTS

A *charitable remainder trust* can provide certain payments to beneficiaries. These payments can be fixed or may be tied to the increase of the asset valuation. They are also can also be an *Income Maximizer Trust* or a *Wealth Replacement Trust.*

An experienced estate planning attorney can help you determine which type of trust will most benefit your needs and goals.

INSURANCE

No discussion about estate planning can go without the discussion of insurance. Upon death the executor contacts the insurance companies regarding payment. If the insurance policy does not provide for a beneficiary or if the beneficiary is the "estate of …" or the primary trust, then the proceeds of the policy goes into the estate. If there is a designated beneficiary the proceeds would go to the beneficiary directly.

Some people believe that insurance policies are a good substitute for a will. One reason this is not true is that by the time of a person's death he or she may have many other assets that would not be covered by the insurance policy. Life insurance is an extremely important asset in building a secure estate plan, but it is only one piece. It should be coordinated with the other documents in your estate.

The last mention here is regarding what is called *Long-Term Insurance*. These are insurance policies that provide for payment if the buyer needs long-term health care. As the buyer ages the probability that he or she will need long-term health care increases and therefore the premiums also increase.

This area of insurance is rather new and can be fraught with pitfalls. As with anything that will affect your future, know what you are buying before you agree to it. Because any insurance policy is a legal contract you may wish to get a legal opinion, before you sign up for any long-term policy.

GOING BEYOND YOUR WILL 13

This book is only a brief overview of the tools that an experienced estate planning attorney will use to help you create the most effective estate to fit your needs. The area of trusts for estate planning is complex and constantly changing with new types of trusts being introduced every year. When the stock market is high, some trusts will be tied to stock investments.

As with any investment, you should consult a licensed investment professional for a proper analysis of this type of trust. In the area of investment trusts, you need to determine the amount you are comfortable risking and the types of investments your estate can handle. There are some unscrupulous estate planners who offer large returns for big investments. Check all such offers out, remember if it sounds too good to be true, it probably is.

As the number of baby boomers increase there will be more tools to help the estate planning attorney and provide clients with options to a simple will. For example, only recently have living trusts been used to provide for pets. The latest subject that is being addressed is long term health care, and the newest tool in this area is insurance, however by the time this book is published there may be other tools to use in planning your estate. Some topics that will probably be addressed in the future are estate planning for those with elderly parents as dependents, estate planning for those in the military, and flexible estate planning for those with multiple divorces.

Estate planning is a very active area, not only must estate planning attorneys have experience, they also must keep up with the new products. If you intend to use an estate planning professional, attorney or investment broker, look for someone who is both experienced and keeps his or her practice current in this area. Ask about his or her attendance at seminars, recent cases effecting wills, pending probate law changes. Most estate planning professionals will enjoy talking about the latest changes or new tools.

GLOSSARY

A

administrator (*administratrix* if female). A person appointed by the court to oversee distribution of the property of someone who died either without a will, or if the person designated in the will is unable to serve.

advance directive. A written document such as a Living Will or a Health Care Power of Attorney which states the medical wishes of person when he/she is unable to speak for him or herself.

agent. A person who you authorize to act for you. You select an agent in the document Health Care Power of Attorney, to speak for you when you are too ill to speak for yourself.

attested will. A will that includes an *attestation clause* and has been signed in front of witnesses.

B

beneficiary. A person who is entitled to receive property from a person who died, regardless of whether there is a will.

bequest. Personal property left to someone in a will.

bond. *See* surety bond.

C

charitable remainder trust. Complex trust, which can provide both a future estate, gift and in some cases a tax deduction.

children's trust. A trust set up to hold property given to children. Usually it provides that the children will not receive their property until they reach a higher age than the age of majority.

codicil. An amendment to a will.

community property. Property acquired by a husband and wife by their labors during their marriage.

D

decedent. A person who has died.

descendent. A child, grandchild, great-grandchild, etc.

devise. Real property left to someone in a will. A person who is entitled to a devise is called a *devisee*.

durable power of attorney. Another name for property power of attorney, or just power of attorney.

E

elective share. In non-community property states, the portion of the estate which may be taken by a surviving spouse, regardless of what the will says.

estate plan. A process where a person's objectives for distribution of his or her property after death are analyzed and legal documents are drawn up to achieve those objectives.

executor (*executrix* if female). A person appointed in a will to oversee distribution of the property of someone who died with a will.

exempt property. Property that is exempt from distribution as a normal part of the estate.

F

family allowance. An amount of money set aside from the estate to support the family of the decedent for a period of time.

forced share. *See* elective share.

G

guardian. Person appointed by a will or court to take care of the property and rights of another person who is unable because of age or capacity to handle their own affairs.

guardianship. The legal term for the duty or authority of a guardian.

H

health care power of attorney. *See* advanced directive.

heir. A person who will inherit from a decedent who died without a will.

holographic will. A will in which all of the material provisions are entirely in the handwriting by the maker. Holographic wills *are not* legal in Illinois.

homestead. Real estate owned by the deceased that is set aside by the probate court for used by the surviving spouse and minor children.

I

income maximizer trust. A type of complex trust which uses investments to increase its value.

intestate. Without making a will. One who dies without a will is said to have *died intestate*.

intestate share. In non-community property states, the portion of the estate a spouse is entitled to receive if there is no will.

ITF. 'In trust for' bank accounts.

J

joint tenancy. A type of property ownership by two or more persons, in which if one owner dies, that owner's interest goes to the other joint tenants (not to the deceased owner's heirs as in tenancy in common).

L

land trust. Allows real property to be put in the name of another for the benefit of a third person.

legacy. Real property left to someone in a will. A person who is entitled to a legacy is called a *legatee.*

living will. A document expressing the writer's desires regarding how medical care is to be handled in the event the writer is not able to express his or her wishes concerning the use of life-prolonging medical procedures.

long-term insurance. The name for insurance to be used for long term health care, primarily for nursing home care.

N

notary public. A person who is licensed to witness that signing of legal documents.

O

opening of an estate. The general term used when a will is filed in the probate court.

P

per capita. Distribution of property with equal shares going to each person.

personal representative. A person appointed by the court or will, to oversee distribution of the property of the person who died. This is a more modern term than "administrator," "executor," etc., and applies regardless of whether there is a will.

per stirpes. Distribution of property with equal shares going to each family line.

power of attorney. A document by which a person appoints another to act as her or his agent in matters of finance, business, or health care.

principal. A person who appoints an agent to act for him or her.

probate. The process of settling a decedent's estate through the probate court.

R

remainder clause. Also called a residuary clause, is the clause in a will which property that was not mentioned specifically in a will is given to the intended beneficiary.

renunciation. Illinois law allows a surviving spouse to renounce what he or she is given in a will for the state-specified percentage of the estate.

residuary clause. *See* remainder clause.

residue. The property that is left over in an estate after all specific bequests and devises.

revocable trust. also called a living trust. Allows the person making the trust to add to or take away from the value of the trusts during his or her lifetime.

S

self-proving affidavit. A form added to a will in which the will maker and witnesses state under oath that they have signed and witnessed the will.

specific bequest *or* **specific devise.** A gift in a will of a specific item of property or a specific amount of cash.

statutory will. A will which has been prepared according to the requirements of a statute.

surety bond. A type of insurance policy that will pay for losses of an executor. An executor would obtain this from an insurance company who would first investigate the executor and then issue the policy for a dollar amount.

T

tenancy by the entirety. A type of property ownership by a married couple, in which the property automatically passes to one spouse upon the death of the other. This is basically the same as joint tenancy, except that it is only between a husband and wife.

tenancy in common. Ownership of property by two or more people, in which each owner's share would descend to that owner's heirs (not to the other owners as in joint tenancy).

testate. With a will. One who dies with a will is said to have *died testate*.

testator. (*testatrix* if female.) A person who makes his or her will.

Totten trust. A trust created by the deposit by one person of his or her own money in his or her own name as a trustee for another person.

trust. Real property, personal property, or anything of value held by one part for the benefit of another.

W

wealth replacement trust. A complex trust that uses investments.

will. Legal document by which a person gives away his or her property after death.

Appendix A
Sample Filled-in Forms

The following pages include sample filled-in forms for some of the wills in this book. They are filled out in different ways for different situations. You should look at all of them to see how the different sections can be filled in. Only one example of a SELF-PROVED WILL AFFIDAVIT is shown, but you should use it with every will.

NOTE: *Attached to each will form as the last page is a* SELF-PROVED WILL AFFIDAVIT. *Although not required by Illinois law, it is a good idea to have one for any will you create.*

Last Will and Testament

I, _____John Doe_____ a resident of _____Lake_____ County, Illinois do hereby make, publish and declare this to be my Last Will and Testament, hereby revoking any and all Wills and Codicils heretofore made by me.

FIRST: I direct that all my just debts and funeral expenses be paid out of my estate as soon after my death as is practicable.

SECOND: I give and bequeath the following personal property unto the following persons:

My gold pocket watch	to James Doe
My antique bookcase	to Sally Doe
	to

THIRD: All the rest, residue and remainder of my estate, real or personal, whereso-ever situate, now owned or hereafter acquired by me, which at the time of my death shall belong to me or be subject to my disposal by will, I give, devise and bequeath unto my spouse, _____Mary Doe_____. If my said spouse does not survive me, I give, and bequeath the said property to my children _____James Doe, Mary Doe, Larry Doe, Barry Doe, Carrie Doe, and Moe Doe_____, plus any afterborn or adopted children in equal shares, or their lineal descendants, per stirpes.

FOURTH: In the event that any beneficiary fails to survive me by thirty days, then this will shall take effect as if that person had predeceased me.

FIFTH: Should my spouse not survive me, I hereby nominate, constitute and appoint _____Sherry Doe_____, as guardian over the person of any of my children who have not reached the age of majority at the time of my death. In the event that said guardian is unable or unwilling to serve then I nominate, constitute and appoint _____Madeleine Doe_____ as guardian. Said guardian to serve without bond or surety.

SIXTH: Should my spouse not survive me, I hereby nominate, constitute and appoint _____Sherry Doe_____ as guardian over the estate of any of my children who have not reached the age of majority at the time of my death. In the event that said guardian is unable or unwilling to serve then I nominate, constitute and appoint _____Englebert Doe_____ as guardian. Said guardian to serve without bond or surety.

SEVENTH: I hereby nominate, constitute and appoint _____Mary Doe_____ to serve as Executor of this, my Last Will and Testament, to serve without bond or surety. In

Initials: **J.D.**   **M.W.**   **W.B.**   Page _1_ of _3_
Testator   Witness   Witness

the event that he or she is unable or unwilling to serve at any time or for any reason then I nominate, constitute and appoint _____Englebert Doe_____ as alternate Executor also to serve without bond or surety. I give my said Executor the fullest power in all matters including the power to sell or convey real or personal property or any interest therein without court order.

IN WITNESS WHEREOF I declare this to be my Last Will and Testament and execute it willingly as my free and voluntary act for the purposes expressed herein and I am of legal age and sound mind and make this under no constraint or undue influence, this 9th day of _____July_____, ___2001___

_____*John Doe*_____

The foregoing instrument was on said date subscribed at the end thereof by _____John Doe_____, the above named Testator who signed, published, and declared this instrument to be his/her Last Will and Testament in the presence of us and each of us, who thereupon at his/her request, in his/her presence, and in the presence of each other, have hereunto subscribed our names as witnesses thereto. We understand this to be his/her will and to the best of our knowledge testator is of legal age, of sound mind and under no constraint or undue influence.

_____*Mickey White*_____residing at 123 Main Street, Chicago, IL

_____*William Black*_____residing at 234 South Street, Chicago, IL

SELF-PROVED WILL PAGE
(attach to Will)

STATE OF ILLINOIS

COUNTY OF _____Lake_____

We, _____John Doe_____, _____Mickey White_____, and _____William Black_____ the testator and the witnesses respectively, whose names are signed to the attached or foregoing instrument, having been sworn, declared to the undersigned officer that the testator, in the presence of witnesses, signed the instrument as his/her last will, that he/she signed, and that each of the witnesses, in the presence of the testator and in the presence of each other, signed the will as witnesses.

John Doe
_____
Testator

Mickey White
_____
Witness

William Black
_____
Witness

Subscribed and sworn to before me by _____John Doe_____ the testator, and by _____Mickey White_____ and _____William Black_____, the witnesses, all of whom personally appeared before me on _____July 9th_____, ___2001___. The testator, _____John Doe_____ is personally known to me or has produced _____ as identification, _____Mickey White_____ is personally known to me or has produced _____ as identification _____William Black_____ is personally known to me or has produced _____ as identification.

C. U. Sine
_____
Notary Public
My commission expires:
My commission number is:

(Notary Seal)

Last Will and Testament

I, _____John Smith_____ a resident of _____Cook_____ County, Illinois do hereby make, publish and declare this to be my Last Will and Testament, hereby revoking any and all Wills and Codicils heretofore made by me.

FIRST: I direct that all my just debts and funeral expenses be paid out of my estate as soon after my death as is practicable.

SECOND: I give and bequeath the following personal property unto the following persons:

my 1968 Ford Mustang	to	my brother Danny Smith
my baseball card collection	to	my sister Sally Small
--------------------	to	--------------------

THIRD: All the rest, residue and remainder of my estate, real or personal, whereso-ever situate, now owned or hereafter acquired by me, which at the time of my death shall belong to me or be subject to my disposal by will, I give, devise and bequeath unto my spouse, _____Barbara Smith_____. If my said spouse does not survive me, I give, and bequeath the said property to my children __Amy Smith, Beamy Smith and Seamy Smith in equal shares__ -- --, in equal shares or to their lineal descendants, per stirpes.

FOURTH: In the event that any beneficiary fails to survive me by thirty days, then this will shall take effect as if that person had predeceased me.

FIFTH: I hereby nominate, constitute and appoint _____Barbara Smith_____ to serve as Executor of this, my Last Will and Testament, to serve without bond or surety. In the event that he or she is unable or unwilling to serve at any time or for any reason then I nominate, constitute and appoint _____Reginald Smith_____ as alternate Executor also to serve without bond or surety. I give my said Executor the fullest power in all matters including the power to sell or convey real or personal property or any interest therein without court order.

IN WITNESS WHEREOF I declare this to be my Last Will and Testament and exe-cute it willingly as my free and voluntary act for the purposes expressed herein and I am of legal age and sound mind and make this under no constraint or undue influence, this __5th__ day of _____January_____, __2002__.

John Smith
_____

The foregoing instrument was on said date subscribed at the end thereof by _____John Smith_____, the above named Testator who signed, pub-lished, and declared this instrument to be his/her Last Will and Testament in the presence of

Initials: __J.S.__ __M.W.__ __W.B.__ Page __1__ of __3__
Testator Witness Witness

us and each of us, who thereupon at his/her request, in his/her presence, and in the presence of each other, have hereunto subscribed our names as witnesses thereto. We understand this to be his/her will and to the best of our knowledge testator is of legal age, of sound mind and under no constraint or undue influence.

_____*Mickey White*_____ residing at _123 Main Street, Chicago, IL_____

_____*William Black*_____ residing at _234 South Street, Chicago, IL_____

Initials: **J.S.**   **M.W.**   **W.B.**   Page _2_ of _3_
        Testator   Witness   Witness

SELF-PROVED WILL PAGE
(attach to Will)

STATE OF ILLINOIS

COUNTY OF ___Cook___

We, ___John Smith___, ___Mickey White___, and
___William Black___ the testator and the witnesses respectively, whose names
are signed to the attached or foregoing instrument, having been sworn, declared to the
undersigned officer that the testator, in the presence of witnesses, signed the instrument as
his/her last will, that he/she signed, and that each of the witnesses, in the presence of the testator and in the presence of each other, signed the will as witnesses.

John Smith
_____
Testator

Mickey White
_____
Witness

William Black
_____
Witness

Subscribed and sworn to before me by ___John Smith___ the testator,
and by ___Mickey White___ and ___William Black___, the witnesses,
all of whom personally appeared before me on ___January 5th___, ___2002___. The
testator, ___John Smith___ is personally known to me or has produced
_____ as identification, ___Mickey White___ is personally known to me or has produced _____ as identification
___William Black___ is personally known to me or has produced
_____ as identification.

C. U. Sine
_____
Notary Public
My commission expires:
My commission number is:

(Notary Seal)

Last Will and Testament

I, _____John Doe_____ a resident of _____Leon_____ County, Illinois do hereby make, publish and declare this to be my Last Will and Testament, hereby revoking any and all Wills and Codicils heretofore made by me.

FIRST: I direct that all my just debts and funeral expenses be paid out of my estate as soon after my death as is practicable.

SECOND: I give and bequeath the following personal property unto the following persons:

My gold pocket watch	to James Smith
My antique bookcase	to Sally Small
	to

THIRD: All the rest, residue and remainder of my estate, real or personal, wheresoever situate, now owned or hereafter acquired by me, which at the time of my death shall belong to me or be subject to my disposal by will, I give, devise and bequeath unto my children James Doe, Mary Doe, Larry Doe, Barry Doe, Carrie Doe, and Moe Doe --- --- _____, plus any afterborn or adopted children in equal shares or to their lineal descendants per stirpes.

FOURTH: In the event that any beneficiary fails to survive me by thirty days, then this will shall take effect as if that person had predeceased me.

FIFTH: In the event that any of my children have not reached the age of __25____ years at the time of my death, then the share of any such child shall be held IN TRUST by _____James Smith_____until such time as such child or children reach the age of ___25___ years. The trustee shall use the income and that part of the principal of the trust as is, in the discretion of the trustee, necessary or desirable to provide proper housing, medical care, food, clothing, entertainment and education for the trust beneficiaries. In the event the said trustee is unable or unwilling to serve for any reason, then I nominate, constitute and appoint ___Sally Small_____as alternate trustee. No bond shall be required of either trustee in any jurisdiction.

SIXTH: In the event any of my children have not attained the age of 18 years at the time of my death, I hereby nominate, constitute and appoint _Sally Small_____ as guardian over the property of any of my children who have not reached the age of majority at the time of my death. In the even that said guardian is unable or unwilling to serve then I nominate, constitute and appoint _Madeleine Small_____ as guardian. Said guardian to serve without bond or surety.

Initials: **J.D.**_____ **M.W.**____ **W.B.**_____   Page _1_ of _3_
  Testator   Witness   Witness

SEVENTH: I hereby nominate, constitute and appoint ___Sally Small___ as Executor of this, my Last Will and Testament. In the event that such named person is unable or unwilling to serve at any time or for any reason then I nominate, constitute and appoint ___Madeleine Small___ as Executor in the place and stead of the person first named herein. It is my will and I direct that my Executor shall not be required to furnish a bond for the faithful performance of his or her duties in any jurisdiction, any provision of law to the contrary notwithstanding and I give my Executor full power to administer my estate, including the power to settle claims, pay debts and sell, lease or exchange real and personal property without court order.

IN WITNESS WHEREOF I declare this to be my Last Will and Testament and execute it willingly as my free and voluntary act for the purposes expressed herein and I am of legal age and sound mind and make this under no constraint or undue influence, this _11th_ day of ___March___, _2002_.

John Doe

The foregoing instrument was on said date subscribed at the end thereof by ___John Doe___, the above named Testator who signed, published, and declared this instrument to be his/her Last Will and Testament in the presence of us and each of us, who thereupon at his/her request, in his/her presence, and in the presence of each other, have hereunto subscribed our names as witnesses thereto. We understand this to be his/her will and to the best of our knowledge testator is of legal age, of sound mind and under no constraint or undue influence.

___*Mickey White*___ residing at ___123 Main Street, Chicago, IL___

___*William Black*___ residing at ___234 South Street, Chicago, IL___

Initials: **J.D.** **M.W.** **W.B.** Page _2_ of _3_
Testator   Witness   Witness

SELF-PROVED WILL PAGE
(attach to Will)

STATE OF ILLINOIS

COUNTY OF _____Leon_____

We, _____John Doe_____, _____Mickey White_____, and _____William Black_____ the testator and the witnesses respectively, whose names are signed to the attached or foregoing instrument, having been sworn, declared to the undersigned officer that the testator, in the presence of witnesses, signed the instrument as his/her last will, that he/she signed, and that each of the witnesses, in the presence of the testator and in the presence of each other, signed the will as witnesses.

John Doe
_____
Testator

Mickey White
_____
Witness

William Black
_____
Witness

Subscribed and sworn to before me by _____John Smith_____ the testator, and by _____Mickey White_____ and _____William Black_____, the witnesses, all of whom personally appeared before me on _____March 11th_____, ___2002___. The testator, _____John Doe_____ is personally known to me or has produced _____ as identification, _____Mickey White_____ is personally known to me or has produced _____ as identification _____William Black_____ is personally known to me or has produced _____ as identification.

C. U. Sine
_____
Notary Public
My commission expires:
My commission number is:

(Notary Seal)

Page _3_ of _3_

Last Will and Testament

I, _____John Smith_____ a resident of _____Cook_____ County, Illinois do hereby make, publish and declare this to be my Last Will and Testament, hereby revoking any and all Wills and Codicils heretofore made by me.

FIRST: I direct that all my just debts and funeral expenses be paid out of my estate as soon after my death as is practicable.

SECOND: I give and bequeath the following personal property unto the following persons:

My gold pocket watch	to	Danny Smith
My antique bookcase	to	Sally Smith
	to	

THIRD: All the rest, residue and remainder of my estate, real or personal, whereso-ever situate, now owned or hereafter acquired by me, which at the time of my death shall belong to me or be subject to my disposal by will, I give, devise and bequeath unto the fol-lowing _____15% to the Cook County Humane Soc.---------_____ 10% to University of Illinois at Chicago----------- 75% to my dear friend, Fannie Farkle, or her lineal descendants, per stirpes--, in equal shares, or their lineal descendants per stirpes.

FOURTH: In the event that any beneficiary fails to survive me by thirty days, then this will shall take effect as if that person had predeceased me.

FIFTH: I hereby nominate, constitute and appoint _____Frannie Farkle_____ to serve as Executor of this, my Last Will and Testament, to serve without bond or surety. In the event that he or she is unable or unwilling to serve at any time or for any reason then I nominate, constitute and appoint _____Danny Smith_____ as alternate Executor also to serve without bond or surety. I give my said Executor the fullest power in all matters including the power to sell or convey real or personal property or any interest therein without court order.

IN WITNESS WHEREOF I declare this to be my Last Will and Testament and exe-cute it willingly as my free and voluntary act for the purposes expressed herein and I am of legal age and sound mind and make this under no constraint or undue influence, this _29th_ day of _January_____, _2001_.

**John Smith**
_____

The foregoing instrument was on said date subscribed at the end thereof by _____John Smith_____, the above named Testator who signed, pub-lished, and declared this instrument to be his/her Last Will and Testament in the presence of us and each of us, who thereupon at his/her request, in his/her presence, and in the presence

Initials: **J.S.**   **M.W.**   **W.B.**   Page _1_ of _3_
    Testator   Witness   Witness

* The second page of this sample form has been omitted.

of us and each of us, who thereupon at his/her request, in his/her presence, and in the presence of each other, have hereunto subscribed our names as witnesses thereto. We understand this to be his/her will and to the best of our knowledge testator is of legal age, of sound mind and under no constraint or undue influence.

_____*Mickey White*_____residing at____123 Main Street, Chicago, IL____

_____*William Black*_____residing at____234 South Street, Chicago, IL____

Initials: **J.S.**   **M.W.**   **W.B.**   Page _2_ of _3_
         Testator   Witness   Witness

SELF-PROVED WILL PAGE
(attach to Will)

STATE OF ILLINOIS

COUNTY OF ___Cook___

We, ___John Smith___, ___Mickey White___, and ___William Black___ the testator and the witnesses respectively, whose names are signed to the attached or foregoing instrument, having been sworn, declared to the undersigned officer that the testator, in the presence of witnesses, signed the instrument as his/her last will, that he/she signed, and that each of the witnesses, in the presence of the testator and in the presence of each other, signed the will as witnesses.

John Smith
_____
Testator

Mickey White
_____
Witness

William Black
_____
Witness

Subscribed and sworn to before me by ___John Smith___ the testator, and by ___Mickey White___ and ___William Black___, the witnesses, all of whom personally appeared before me on ___January 29th___, ___2001___. The testator, ___John Smith___ is personally known to me or has produced _____ as identification, ___Mickey White___ is personally known to me or has produced _____ as identification ___William Black___ is personally known to me or has produced _____ as identification.

C. U. Sine
_____
Notary Public
My commission expires:
My commission number is:

(Notary Seal)

Codicil to the Will of

<u>Larry Lowe</u>

I, _____<u>Larry Lowe</u>_____, a resident of _____<u>Cook</u>_____ County, Illinois declare this to be the first codicil to my Last Will and Testament dated ____<u>July 5</u>____, <u>2001</u>.

FIRST: I hereby revoke the clause of my Will which reads as follows: _____
<u>FOURTH: I hereby leave $5000.00 to my daughter Mildred</u> _____

SECOND: I hereby add following clause to my Will: _____
<u>FOURTH: I hereby leave $1000.00 to my daughter Mildred</u> _____

THIRD: In all other respects I hereby confirm and republish my Last Will and Testament dated <u>July 5</u>, <u>1999</u>.

Date: <u>January 15, 2000</u>   *Larry Lowe*
                                      _____

We, the undersigned persons, of lawful age, have on this <u>5th</u> day of ____<u>July</u>____, <u>2001</u>, at the request of _____<u>Larry Lowe</u>_____, witnessed his/her signature to the foregoing First Codicil to Will in the presence of each of us; and we have, at the same time and in his/her presence and in the presence of each other, subscribed our names hereto as attesting witnesses.

Michael Smith
_____ residing at: ____<u>21 Oak Lane</u>____
                                      <u>Chicago, IL 60657</u>

Mary Smith
_____ residing at: ____<u>502 W. Briar</u>____
                                      <u>Chicago, IL 60657</u>

SELF-PROVING AFFIDAVIT

STATE OF ILLINOIS   §
                              §
COUNTY OF _____<u>Cook</u>_____   §

We, _____<u>Larry Lowe</u>_____ and _____<u>Mary Smith</u>_____ and <u>Michael Smith</u>, the testator and the witnesses, whose names are signed to the attached or foregoing instrument in those capacities, personally appearing before the undersigned authority and being first duly sworn, declare to the undersigned authority under penalty of perjury that: 1) the testator declared, signed and executed the instrument as his or her last will; 2) he or she signed it willingly or directed another to sign for him or her; 3) he or she executed it as his or her free and voluntary act for the purposes therein expressed; and 4) each of the witnesses, and the request of the testator, in his or her hearing and presence and in the presence of each other, signed the will as witnesses and that to the best of his or her knowledge the testator was at that time of full legal age, of sound mind and under no constraint or undue influence.

Larry Lowe   *Michael Smith*
_____   _____
TESTATOR   WITNESS

                               Mary Smith
                               _____
                               WITNESS

SUBSCRIBED AND ACKNOWLEDGED before me by ____<u>Larry Lowe</u>____, the Testator and subscribed and sworn to before me by the above-named witnesses this <u>5th</u> day of____<u>July</u>____, <u>2001</u>.

                               Arthur Izer
                               _____
                               Notary Public
                               Page <u>1</u> of <u>1</u>

LIVING WILL DECLARATION

This declaration is made this ___5th___ day of _____January 2002_____ (month, year). I, _____John Smith_____, being of sound mind, willfully and voluntarily make known my desires that my moment of death shall not be artificially postponed.

If at any time I should have an incurable and irreversible injury, disease, or illness judged to be a terminal condition by my attending physician who has personally examined me and has determined that my death is imminent except for death delaying procedures, I direct that such procedures which would only prolong the dying process be withheld or withdrawn, and that I be permitted to die naturally with only the administration of medication, sustenance, or the performance of any medical procedure deemed necessary by my attending physician to provide me with comfort care.

In the absence of my ability to give directions regarding the use of such death delaying procedures, it is my intention that this declaration shall be honored by my family and physician as the final expression of my legal right to refuse medical or surgical treatment and accept the consequences from such refusal.

Signed _____*John Smith*_____

City, County and State of Residence _____Chicago, Cook County, Illinois_____

The declarant is personally known to me and I believe him or her to be of sound mind. I saw the declarant sign the declaration in my presence (or the declarant acknowledged in my presence that he or she had signed the declaration) and I signed the declaration as a witness in the presence of the declarant. I did not sign the declarant's signature above for or at the direction of the declarant. At the date of this instrument, I am not entitled to any portion of the estate of the declarant according to the laws of intestate succession or, to the best of my knowledge and belief, under any will or declarant or other instrument taking effect at declarant's death, or directly financially responsible for declarant's medical care.

Witness _____*Michael Jones*_____

Witness _____*Mary Jones*_____

Page _1_ of _1_

ILLINOIS STATUTORY SHORT FORM POWER OF ATTORNEY FOR HEALTH CARE

(NOTICE: THE PURPOSE OF THIS POWER OF ATTORNEY IS TO GIVE THE PERSON YOU DESIGNATE (YOUR "AGENT") BROAD POWERS TO MAKE HEALTH CARE DECISIONS FOR YOU, INCLUDING POWER TO REQUIRE, CONSENT TO OR WITHDRAW ANY TYPE OF PERSONAL CARE OR MEDICAL TREATMENT FOR ANY PHYSICAL OR MENTAL CONDITION AND TO ADMIT YOU TO OR DISCHARGE YOU FROM ANY HOSPITAL, HOME OR OTHER INSTITUTION. THIS FORM DOES NOT IMPOSE A DUTY ON YOUR AGENT TO EXERCISE GRANTED POWERS; BUT WHEN POWERS ARE EXERCISED, YOUR AGENT WILL HAVE TO USE DUE CARE TO ACT FOR YOUR BENEFIT AND IN ACCORDANCE WITH THIS FORM AND KEEP A RECORD OF RECEIPTS, DISBURSEMENTS AND SIGNIFICANT ACTIONS TAKEN AS AGENT. A COURT CAN TAKE AWAY THE POWERS OF YOUR AGENT IF IT FINDS THE AGENT IS NOT ACTING PROPERLY. YOU MAY NAME SUCCESSOR AGENTS UNDER THIS FORM BUT NOT CO-AGENTS, AND NO HEALTH CARE PROVIDER MAY BE NAMED. UNLESS YOU EXPRESSLY LIMIT THE DURATION OF THIS POWER IN THE MANNER PROVIDED BELOW, UNTIL YOU REVOKE THIS POWER OR A COURT ACTING ON YOUR BEHALF TERMINATES IT, YOUR AGENT MAY EXERCISE THE POWERS GIVEN HERE THROUGHOUT YOUR LIFETIME, EVEN AFTER YOU BECOME DISABLED. THE POWERS YOU GIVE YOUR AGENT, YOUR RIGHT TO REVOKE THOSE POWERS AND THE PENALTIES FOR VIOLATING THE LAW ARE EXPLAINED MORE FULLY IN SECTIONS 4-5, 4-6, 4-9 AND 4-10(b) OF THE ILLINOIS "POWERS OF ATTORNEY FOR HEALTH CARE LAW" OF WHICH THIS FORM IS A PART (SEE THE BACK OF THIS FORM). THAT LAW EXPRESSLY PERMITS THE USE OF ANY DIFFERENT FORM OF POWER OF ATTORNEY YOU MAY DESIRE. IF THERE IS ANYTHING ABOUT THIS FORM THAT YOU DO NOT UNDERSTAND, YOU SHOULD ASK A LAWYER TO EXPLAIN IT TO YOU.)

POWER OF ATTORNEY made this ____22nd____ day of _____May_____ __2001__
                                                    (month)   (year)

1. I, ____John Smith____
      126 Main Street, Itaska, Illinois
            (insert name and address of principal)

hereby appoint:
      Barbara Smith
      126 Main Street, Itaska, Illinois
            (insert name and address of agent)

as my attorney-in-fact (my "agent") to act for me and in my name (in any way I could act in person) to make any and all decisions for me concerning my personal care, medical treatment, hospitalization and health care and to require, withhold or withdraw any type of medical treatment or procedure, even though my death may ensue. My agent shall have the same access to my medical records that I have, including the right to disclose the contents to others. My agent shall also have full power to make a disposition of any part or all of my body for medical purposes, authorize an autopsy and direct the disposition of my remains.

(THE ABOVE GRANT OF POWER IS INTENDED TO BE AS BROAD AS POSSIBLE SO THAT YOUR AGENT WILL HAVE AUTHORITY TO MAKE ANY DECISION YOU COULD MAKE TO OBTAIN OR TERMINATE ANY TYPE OF HEALTH CARE, INCLUDING WITHDRAWAL OF FOOD AND WATER AND OTHER LIFE-SUSTAINING MEASURES, IF YOUR AGENT BELIEVES SUCH ACTION WOULD BE CONSISTENT WITH YOUR INTENT AND DESIRES. IF YOU WISH TO LIMIT THE SCOPE OF YOUR AGENT'S POWERS OR PRESCRIBE SPECIAL RULES OR LIMIT THE POWER TO MAKE AN ANATOMICAL GIFT, AUTHORIZE AUTOPSY OR DISPOSE OF REMAINS, YOU MAY DO SO IN THE FOLLOWING PARAGRAPHS.)

2. The powers granted above shall not include the following powers or shall be subject to the following rules or limitations (here you may include any specific limitations you deem appropriate, such as: your own definition of when life-sustaining measures should be withheld; a direction to continue food and fluids or life-sustaining treatment in all events; or instructions to refuse any specific types of treatment that are inconsistent with your religious beliefs or unacceptable to you for any other reason, such as blood transfusion, electro-convulsive therapy, amputation, psychosurgery, voluntary admission to a mental institution, etc.): ____no limitations____

(THE SUBJECT OF LIFE-SUSTAINING TREATMENT IS OF PARTICULAR IMPORTANCE. FOR YOUR CONVENIENCE IN DEALING WITH THAT SUBJECT, SOME GENERAL STATEMENTS CONCERNING THE WITHHOLDING OR REMOVAL OF LIFE-SUSTAINING TREATMENT ARE SET FORTH BELOW. IF YOU AGREE WITH ONE OF THESE STATEMENTS, YOU MAY INITIAL THAT STATEMENT; BUT DO NOT INITIAL MORE THAN ONE):

I do not want my life to be prolonged nor do I want life-sustaining treatment to be provided or continued if my agent believes the burdens of the treatment outweigh the expected benefits. I want my agent to consider the relief of suffering, the expense involved and the quality as well as the possible extension of my life in making decisions concerning life sustaining treatment.

Initialed ____**J.S.**____

Page _1_ of _2_

I want my life to be prolonged and I want life-sustaining treatment to be provided or continued unless I am in a coma which my attending physician believes to be irreversible, in accordance with reasonable medical standards at the time of reference. If and when I have suffered irreversible coma, I want life-sustaining treatment to be withheld or discontinued.

Initialed _____

I want my life to be prolonged to the greatest extent possible without regard to my condition, the chances I have for recovery or the cost of the procedures.

Initialed _____

(THIS POWER OF ATTORNEY MAY BE AMENDED OR REVOKED BY YOU IN THE MANNER PROVIDED IN SECTION 4-6 OF THE ILLINOIS "POWERS OF ATTORNEY FOR HEALTH CARE LAW" (SEE THE BACK OF THIS FORM). ABSENT AMENDMENT OR REVOCATION, THE AUTHORITY GRANTED IN THIS POWER OF ATTORNEY WILL BECOME EFFECTIVE AT THE TIME THIS POWER IS SIGNED AND WILL CONTINUE UNTIL YOUR DEATH, AND BEYOND IF ANATOMICAL GIFT, AUTOPSY OR DISPOSITION OF REMAINS IS AUTHORIZED, UNLESS A LIMITATION ON THE BEGINNING DATE OR DURATION IS MADE BY INITIALING AND COMPLETING EITHER OR BOTH OF THE FOLLOWING:)

3. (*J.S.*) This power of attorney shall become effective on -- _____ immediately _____

_____(insert a future date or event during your lifetime, such as court determination of your disability, when you want this power to first take effect)

4. (_____) This power of attorney shall terminate on_____

_____(insert a future date or event, such as court determination of your disability, when you want this power to terminate prior to your death)

(IF YOU WISH TO NAME SUCCESSOR AGENTS, INSERT THE NAMES AND ADDRESSES OF SUCH SUCCESSORS IN THE FOLLOWING PARAGRAPH.)

5. If any agent named by me shall die, become incompetent, resign, refuse to accept the office of agent or be unavailable, I name the following (each to act alone and successively, in the order named) as successors to such agent:___John Smith, Jr. 9401 Hancock Building, Chicago, Illinois_____

_____

For purposes of this paragraph 5, a person shall be considered to be incompetent if and while the person is a minor or an adjudicated incompetent or disabled person or the person is unable to give prompt and intelligent consideration to health care matters, as certified by a licensed physician.

(IF YOU WISH TO NAME YOUR AGENT AS GUARDIAN OF YOUR PERSON, IN THE EVENT A COURT DECIDES THAT ONE SHOULD BE APPOINTED, YOU MAY, BUT ARE NOT REQUIRED TO, DO SO BY RETAINING THE FOLLOWING PARAGRAPH. THE COURT WILL APPOINT YOUR AGENT IF THE COURT FINDS THAT SUCH APPOINTMENT WILL SERVE YOUR BEST INTERESTS AND WELFARE. STRIKE OUT PARAGRAPH 6 IF YOU DO NOT WANT YOUR AGENT TO ACT AS GUARDIAN.)

6. If a guardian of my person is to be appointed, I nominate the agent acting under this power of attorney as such guardian, to serve without bond or security. (insert name and address of nominated guardian of the person)

7. I am fully informed as to all the contents of this form and understand the full import of this grant of powers to my agent.

Signed _____*John Smith*_____
(principal)

The principal has had an opportunity to read the above form and has signed the form or acknowledged his or her signature or mark on the form in my presence.

*Charles Doe*_____   Residing at ___128 Main Street_____
(witness)   ___Itaska, Illinois_____

(YOU MAY, BUT ARE NOT REQUIRED TO, REQUEST YOUR AGENT AND SUCCESSOR AGENTS TO PROVIDE SPECIMEN SIGNATURES BELOW. IF YOU INCLUDE SPECIMEN SIGNATURES IN THIS POWER OF ATTORNEY YOU MUST COMPLETE THE CERTIFICATION OPPOSITE THE SIGNATURES OF THE AGENTS.)

Specimen signatures of agent (and successors).   I certify that the signatures of my agent (and successors) are correct

*Mary Smith*_____   *John Smith*_____
(agent)   (principal)

*John Smith, Jr.*_____   *John Smith*_____
(successor agent)   (principal)

_____   _____
(successor agent)   (principal)

Page __2__ of __2__

90

Appendix B
Blank Forms

The following pages contain forms which can be used to prepare a will, codicil, living will, and Uniform Donor Card. They should only be used by persons who have read this book, who do not have any complications in their legal affairs and who understand the forms they are using. The forms may be used right out of the book or they may be photocopied or retyped.

NOTE: *Attached to each will form as the last page is a* SELF-PROVED WILL AFFIDAVIT. *Although not required by Illinois law, it is a good idea to have one for any will you create.*

How to Pick the Right Will

You can follow this chart to find the right will for your situation.
Then use form 17 for the self-proved affidavit.

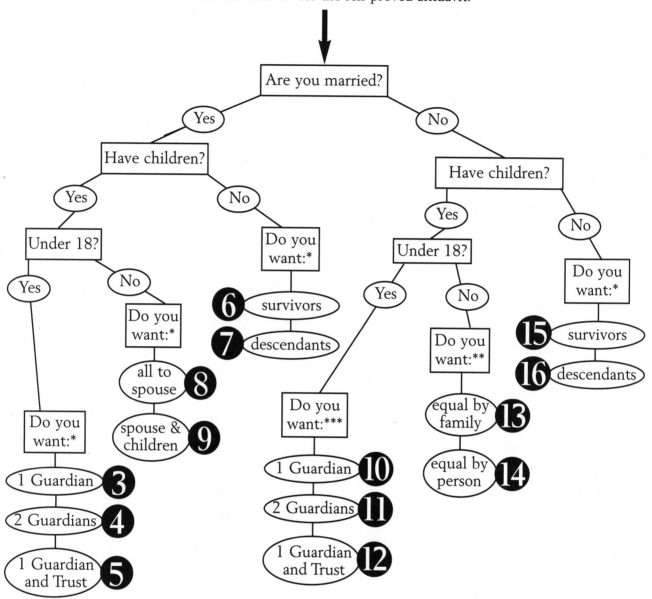

17 Use the self-proving affidavit with all wills

* For an explanation of survivors/descendants, see pages 36-38.
** For an explanation of families/persons, see pages 36-38.
*** For an explanation of children's guardians and trust, see pages 39-40.

Asset and Beneficiary List

Property Inventory

Assets

Bank Accounts (checking, savings, certificates of deposit)

_____

_____

_____

_____

_____

_____

_____

_____

Real estate

_____

_____

_____

_____

_____

_____

_____

_____

Vehicles (cars, trucks, boats, planes, RVs, etc.)

_____

_____

_____

_____

_____

_____

_____

_____

Personal Property (collections, jewelry, tools, artwork, household items, etc.)

_____

_____

_____

_____

_____

_____

_____

_____

_____

_____

_____

_____

_____

_____

_____

Stocks/Bonds/Mutual Funds

_____

_____

_____

_____

_____

_____

_____

_____

_____

_____

_____

_____

_____

Retirement Accounts (IRAs, 401(k)s, pension plans, etc.)

_____

_____

_____

_____

_____

_____

_____

Receivables (mortgages held, notes, accounts receivable, personal loans)

_____

_____

_____

_____

_____

_____

_____

_____

Life insurance

_____

_____

_____

_____

_____

_____

Other property (trusts, partnerships, businesses, profit sharing, copyrights, etc.)

_____

_____

_____

_____

_____

_____

_____

Liabilities

Real Estate Loans

_____

_____

_____

_____

_____

_____

Vehicle Loans

_____

_____

_____

_____

_____

_____

Other Secured Loans

_____
_____
_____
_____
_____
_____
_____

Unsecured Loans and Debts (taxes, child support, judgments, etc.)

_____
_____
_____
_____
_____
_____
_____

Beneficiary List

Name_____ Address_____ Phone_____

Name_____ Address_____ Phone_____

Name_____ Address_____ Phone_____

Name_____ Address_____ Phone_____

Name_____ Address_____ Phone_____

Preferences List

STATEMENT OF DESIRES AND LOCATION OF PROPERTY & DOCUMENTS

I, _____, am signing this document as the expression of my desires as to the matters stated below, and to inform my family members or other significant persons of the location of certain property and documents in the event of any emergency or of my death.

1. **Funeral Desires.** It is my desire that the following arrangements be made for my funeral and disposition of remains in the event of my death (state if you have made any arrangements, such as pre-paid burial plans, cemetery plots owned, etc.):

    ❑   Burial at _____
    _____.

    ❑   Cremation at _____
    _____.

    ❑   Other specific desires: _____
    _____
    _____.

2. **Pets.** I have the following pet(s): _____
    _____. The following are my desires concerning the care of said pet(s): _____
    _____
    _____.

4. **Notification.** I would like the following person(s) notified in the event of emergency or death (give name, address and phone number):

    _____
    _____
    _____
    _____.

5. **Location of Documents.** The following is a list of important documents, and their location:

    ❑   Last Will and Testament, dated _____. Location: _____
    _____.

    ❑   Durable Power of Attorney, dated _____. Location: _____
    _____.

    ❑   Living Will, dated _____. Location: _____
    _____.

    ❑   Deed(s) to real estate (describe property location and location of deed):
    _____
    _____
    _____

❑ Title(s) to vehicles (cars, boats, etc.) (Describe vehicle, its location, and location of title, registration, or other documents):

_____
_____
_____
_____

❑ Life insurance policies (list name address & phone number of insurance company and insurance agent, policy number, and location of policy):

_____
_____
_____

❑ Other insurance policies (list type, company & agent, policy number, and location of policy):

_____
_____
_____

❑ Other: (list other documents such as stock certificates, bonds, certificates of deposit, etc., and their location):

_____
_____
_____

6.   **Location of Assets.** In addition to items readily visible in my home or listed above, I have the following assets:

❑ Safe deposit box located at _____, box number _____. Key located at: _____.

❑ Bank accounts (list name & address of bank, type of account, and account number):

_____

❑ Other (describe the item and give its location):

_____
_____
_____
_____

7.   Other desires or information (state any desires or provide any information not given above; use additional sheets of paper if necessary):

_____
_____
_____
_____
_____

Dated: _____

_____
Signature

Last Will and Testament

I, _____ a resident of _____
County, Illinois do hereby make, publish and declare this to be my Last Will and Testament, hereby revoking any and all Wills and Codicils heretofore made by me.

FIRST: I direct that all my just debts and funeral expenses be paid out of my estate as soon after my death as is practicable.

SECOND: I give and bequeath the following personal property unto the following persons:

_____ to _____
_____ to _____
_____ to _____

THIRD: All the rest, residue and remainder of my estate, real or personal, whereso-ever situate, now owned or hereafter acquired by me, which at the time of my death shall belong to me or be subject to my disposal by will, I give, devise and bequeath unto my spouse, _____. If my said spouse does not survive me, I give, and bequeath the said property to my children _____
_____
_____,
plus any afterborn or adopted children in equal shares, or their lineal descendants, per stirpes.

FOURTH: In the event that any beneficiary fails to survive me by thirty days, then this will shall take effect as if that person had predeceased me.

FIFTH: Should my spouse not survive me, I hereby nominate, constitute and appoint _____ as guardian over the person and estate of any of my children who have not reached the age of majority at the time of my death. In the even that said guardian is unable or unwilling to serve then I nominate, constitute and appoint _____ as guardian. Said guardian to serve without bond or surety.

SIXTH: I hereby nominate, constitute and appoint _____ to serve as Executor of this, my Last Will and Testament, to serve without bond or surety. In the event that he or she is unable or unwilling to serve at any time or for any reason then I nominate, constitute and appoint _____ as alternate Executor also to serve without bond or surety. I give my said Executor the fullest power in all matters including the power to sell or convey real or personal property or any interest therein with-out court order.

Initials: _____ _____ _____   Page ____ of ____
          Testator   Witness   Witness

IN WITNESS WHEREOF I declare this to be my Last Will and Testament and execute it willingly as my free and voluntary act for the purposes expressed herein and I am of legal age and sound mind and make this under no constraint or undue influence, this _____ day of _____, _____.

_____

The foregoing instrument was on said date subscribed at the end thereof by _____, the above named Testator who signed, published, and declared this instrument to be his/her Last Will and Testament in the presence of us and each of us, who thereupon at his/her request, in his/her presence, and in the presence of each other, have hereunto subscribed our names as witnesses thereto. We understand this to be his/her will and to the best of our knowledge testator is of legal age, of sound mind and under no constraint or undue influence.

_____residing at_____

_____residing at_____

Page _____ of _____

SELF-PROVED WILL PAGE
(attach to Will)

STATE OF ILLINOIS

COUNTY OF _____

We, _____, _____, and
_____ the testator and the witnesses respectively, whose names
are signed to the attached or foregoing instrument, having been sworn, declared to the
undersigned officer that the testator, in the presence of witnesses, signed the instrument as
his/her last will, that he/she signed, and that each of the witnesses, in the presence of the testator and in the presence of each other, signed the will as witnesses.

_____
Testator

_____
Witness

_____
Witness

Subscribed and sworn to before me by _____ the testator,
and by _____ and _____, the witnesses,
all of whom personally appeared before me on _____, _____. The
testator, _____ is personally known to me or has produced
_____ as identification, _____ is personally known to me or has produced _____ as identification
_____ is personally known to me or has produced
_____ as identification.

_____
Notary Public
My commission expires:
My commission number is:

(Notary Seal)

Page _____ of _____

This page intentionally left blank.

Last Will and Testament

I, _____ a resident of _____ County, Illinois do hereby make, publish and declare this to be my Last Will and Testament, hereby revoking any and all Wills and Codicils heretofore made by me.

FIRST: I direct that all my just debts and funeral expenses be paid out of my estate as soon after my death as is practicable.

SECOND: I give and bequeath the following personal property unto the following persons:

_____ to _____
_____ to _____
_____ to _____

THIRD: All the rest, residue and remainder of my estate, real or personal, whereso-ever situate, now owned or hereafter acquired by me, which at the time of my death shall belong to me or be subject to my disposal by will, I give, devise and bequeath unto my spouse, _____. If my said spouse does not survive me, I give, and bequeath the said property to my children _____ _____ _____, plus any afterborn or adopted children in equal shares, or their lineal descendants, per stirpes.

FOURTH: In the event that any beneficiary fails to survive me by thirty days, then this will shall take effect as if that person had predeceased me.

FIFTH: Should my spouse not survive me, I hereby nominate, constitute and appoint _____, as guardian over the person of any of my children who have not reached the age of majority at the time of my death. In the event that said guardian is unable or unwilling to serve then I nominate, constitute and appoint _____ as guardian. Said guardian to serve without bond or surety.

SIXTH: Should my spouse not survive me, I hereby nominate, constitute and appoint _____ as guardian over the estate of any of my children who have not reached the age of majority at the time of my death. In the event that said guardian is unable or unwilling to serve then I nominate, constitute and appoint _____ _____ as guardian. Said guardian to serve without bond or surety.

SEVENTH: I hereby nominate, constitute and appoint _____ to serve as Executor of this, my Last Will and Testament, to serve without bond or surety. In

Initials: _____ _____ _____   Page ____ of ____
       Testator   Witness   Witness

the event that he or she is unable or unwilling to serve at any time or for any reason then I nominate, constitute and appoint _____ as alternate Executor also to serve without bond or surety. I give my said Executor the fullest power in all matters including the power to sell or convey real or personal property or any interest therein without court order.

IN WITNESS WHEREOF I declare this to be my Last Will and Testament and execute it willingly as my free and voluntary act for the purposes expressed herein and I am of legal age and sound mind and make this under no constraint or undue influence, this _____ day of _____, _____.

_____

The foregoing instrument was on said date subscribed at the end thereof by _____, the above named Testator who signed, published, and declared this instrument to be his/her Last Will and Testament in the presence of us and each of us, who thereupon at his/her request, in his/her presence, and in the presence of each other, have hereunto subscribed our names as witnesses thereto. We understand this to be his/her will and to the best of our knowledge testator is of legal age, of sound mind and under no constraint or undue influence.

_____residing at_____

_____residing at_____

Page _____ of _____

106

SELF-PROVED WILL PAGE
(attach to Will)

STATE OF ILLINOIS

COUNTY OF _____

We, _____, _____, and _____ the testator and the witnesses respectively, whose names are signed to the attached or foregoing instrument, having been sworn, declared to the undersigned officer that the testator, in the presence of witnesses, signed the instrument as his/her last will, that he/she signed, and that each of the witnesses, in the presence of the testator and in the presence of each other, signed the will as witnesses.

_____
Testator

_____
Witness

_____
Witness

Subscribed and sworn to before me by _____ the testator, and by _____ and _____, the witnesses, all of whom personally appeared before me on _____, _____. The testator, _____ is personally known to me or has produced _____ as identification, _____ is personally known to me or has produced _____ as identification _____ is personally known to me or has produced _____ as identification.

_____
Notary Public
My commission expires:
My commission number is:

(Notary Seal)

Page _____ of _____

107

This page intentionally left blank.

Last Will and Testament

I, _____ a resident of _____ County, Illinois do hereby make, publish and declare this to be my Last Will and Testament, hereby revoking any and all Wills and Codicils heretofore made by me.

FIRST: I direct that all my just debts and funeral expenses be paid out of my estate as soon after my death as is practicable.

SECOND: I give and bequeath the following personal property unto the following persons:

_____ to _____
_____ to _____
_____ to _____

THIRD: All the rest, residue and remainder of my estate, real or personal, whereso-ever situate, now owned or hereafter acquired by me, which at the time of my death shall belong to me or be subject to my disposal by will, I give, devise and bequeath unto my spouse, _____. If my said spouse does not survive me, I give, and bequeath the said property to my children _____

_____

_____,

plus any afterborn or adopted children in equal shares, or their lineal descendants, per stirpes.

FOURTH: In the event that any beneficiary fails to survive me by thirty days, then this will shall take effect as if that person had predeceased me.

FIFTH: In the event that any of my children have not reached the age of _____ years at the time of my death, then the share of any such child shall be held in a separate trust by _____ for such child.

The trustee shall use the income and that part of the principal of the trust as is, in the trustee's sole discretion, necessary or desirable to provide proper housing, medical care, food, clothing, entertainment and education for the trust beneficiary, considering the beneficiary's other resources. Any income that is not distributed shall be added to the principal. Additionally, the trustee shall have all powers conferred by the law of the state having juris-diction over this trust, as well as the power to pay from the assets of the trust reasonable fees necessary to administer the trust.

The trust shall terminate when the child reaches the age specified above and the remaining assets distributed to the child, unless they have been exhausted sooner. In the event the child dies prior to the termination of the trust, then the assets shall pass to the estate of the child.

Initials: _____ _____ _____   Page ____ of ____
          Testator   Witness   Witness

109

The interests of the beneficiary under this trust shall not be assignable and shall be free from the claims of creditors to the full extent allowed by law.

In the event the said trustee is unable or unwilling to serve for any reason, then I nominate, constitute, and appoint _____as alternate trustee. No bond shall be required of either trustee in any jurisdiction and this trust shall be administered without court supervision as allowed by law.

SIXTH: Should my spouse not survive me, I hereby nominate, constitute and appoint_____as guardian over the person and estate of any of my children who have not reached the age of majority at the time of my death. In the even that said guardian is unable or unwilling to serve then I nominate, constitute and appoint_____ as guardian.

SEVENTH: I hereby nominate, constitute and appoint _____ to serve as Executor of this, my Last Will and Testament, to serve without bond or surety. In the event that he or she is unable or unwilling to serve at any time or for any reason then I nominate, constitute and appoint _____ as alternate Executor also to serve without bond or surety. I give my said Executor the fullest power in all matters including the power to sell or convey real or personal property or any interest therein without court order.

IN WITNESS WHEREOF I declare this to be my Last Will and Testament and execute it willingly as my free and voluntary act for the purposes expressed herein and I am of legal age and sound mind and make this under no constraint or undue influence, this _____ day of _____, _____.

_____

The foregoing instrument was on said date subscribed at the end thereof by _____, the above named Testator who signed, published, and declared this instrument to be his/her Last Will and Testament in the presence of us and each of us, who thereupon at his/her request, in his/her presence, and in the presence of each other, have hereunto subscribed our names as witnesses thereto. We understand this to be his/her will and to the best of our knowledge testator is of legal age, of sound mind and under no constraint or undue influence.

_____residing at_____

_____residing at_____

Page ____ of ____

SELF-PROVED WILL PAGE
(attach to Will)

STATE OF ILLINOIS

COUNTY OF _____

    We, _____, _____, and
_____ the testator and the witnesses respectively, whose names
are signed to the attached or foregoing instrument, having been sworn, declared to the
undersigned officer that the testator, in the presence of witnesses, signed the instrument as
his/her last will, that he/she signed, and that each of the witnesses, in the presence of the testator and in the presence of each other, signed the will as witnesses.

                                      _____
                                      Testator

                                      _____
                                      Witness

                                      _____
                                      Witness

    Subscribed and sworn to before me by _____ the testator,
and by _____ and _____, the witnesses,
all of whom personally appeared before me on _____, _____. The
testator, _____ is personally known to me or has produced
_____ as identification, _____ is personally known to me or has produced _____ as identification
_____ is personally known to me or has produced
_____ as identification.

                                      _____
                                      Notary Public
                                      My commission expires:
                                      My commission number is:

(Notary Seal)

Page _____ of _____

This page intentionally left blank.

Last Will and Testament

I, _____ a resident of _____ County, Illinois do hereby make, publish and declare this to be my Last Will and Testament, hereby revoking any and all Wills and Codicils heretofore made by me.

FIRST: I direct that all my just debts and funeral expenses be paid out of my estate as soon after my death as is practicable.

SECOND: I give and bequeath the following personal property unto the following persons:

_____ to _____
_____ to _____
_____ to _____

THIRD: All the rest, residue and remainder of my estate, real or personal, wheresoever situate, now owned or hereafter acquired by me, which at the time of my death shall belong to me or be subject to my disposal by will, I give, devise and bequeath unto my spouse, _____. If my said spouse does not survive me, I give, and bequeath the said property to _____ _____ _____, or the survivor of them.

FOURTH: In the event that any beneficiary fails to survive me by thirty days, then this will shall take effect as if that person had predeceased me.

FIFTH: I hereby nominate, constitute and appoint _____ to serve as Executor of this, my Last Will and Testament, to serve without bond or surety. In the event that he or she is unable or unwilling to serve at any time or for any reason then I nominate, constitute and appoint _____ as alternate Executor also to serve without bond or surety. I give my said Executor the fullest power in all matters including the power to sell or convey real or personal property or any interest therein without court order.

Initials: _____ _____ _____   Page ____ of ____
           Testator   Witness   Witness

IN WITNESS WHEREOF I declare this to be my Last Will and Testament and execute it willingly as my free and voluntary act for the purposes expressed herein and I am of legal age and sound mind and make this under no constraint or undue influence, this _____ day of _____, _____.

_____

The foregoing instrument was on said date subscribed at the end thereof by _____, the above named Testator who signed, published, and declared this instrument to be his/her Last Will and Testament in the presence of us and each of us, who thereupon at his/her request, in his/her presence, and in the presence of each other, have hereunto subscribed our names as witnesses thereto. We understand this to be his/her will and to the best of our knowledge testator is of legal age, of sound mind and under no constraint or undue influence.

_____residing at_____

_____residing at_____

Page _____ of _____

SELF-PROVED WILL PAGE
(attach to Will)

STATE OF ILLINOIS

COUNTY OF _____

    We, _____, _____, and _____ the testator and the witnesses respectively, whose names are signed to the attached or foregoing instrument, having been sworn, declared to the undersigned officer that the testator, in the presence of witnesses, signed the instrument as his/her last will, that he/she signed, and that each of the witnesses, in the presence of the testator and in the presence of each other, signed the will as witnesses.

_____
Testator

_____
Witness

_____
Witness

    Subscribed and sworn to before me by _____ the testator, and by _____ and _____, the witnesses, all of whom personally appeared before me on _____, _____. The testator, _____ is personally known to me or has produced _____ as identification, _____ is personally known to me or has produced _____ as identification _____ is personally known to me or has produced _____ as identification.

_____
Notary Public
My commission expires:
My commission number is:

(Notary Seal)

Page ____ of ____

115

This page intentionally left blank.

Last Will and Testament

I, _____ a resident of _____
County, Illinois do hereby make, publish and declare this to be my Last Will and Testament, hereby revoking any and all Wills and Codicils heretofore made by me.

FIRST: I direct that all my just debts and funeral expenses be paid out of my estate as soon after my death as is practicable.

SECOND: I give and bequeath the following personal property unto the following persons:

_____ to _____
_____ to _____
_____ to _____

THIRD: All the rest, residue and remainder of my estate, real or personal, wheresoever situate, now owned or hereafter acquired by me, which at the time of my death shall belong to me or be subject to my disposal by will, I give, devise and bequeath unto my spouse, _____. If my said spouse does not survive me, I give, and bequeath the said property to _____
_____
_____,
or to their lineal descendants, per stirpes.

FOURTH: In the event that any beneficiary fails to survive me by thirty days, then this will shall take effect as if that person had predeceased me.

FIFTH: I hereby nominate, constitute and appoint _____ to serve as Executor of this, my Last Will and Testament, to serve without bond or surety. In the event that he or she is unable or unwilling to serve at any time or for any reason then I nominate, constitute and appoint _____ as alternate Executor also to serve without bond or surety. I give my said Executor the fullest power in all matters including the power to sell or convey real or personal property or any interest therein without court order.

Initials: _____ _____ _____   Page ____ of ____
         Testator   Witness   Witness

IN WITNESS WHEREOF I declare this to be my Last Will and Testament and execute it willingly as my free and voluntary act for the purposes expressed herein and I am of legal age and sound mind and make this under no constraint or undue influence, this _____ day of _____, _____.

_____

The foregoing instrument was on said date subscribed at the end thereof by _____, the above named Testator who signed, published, and declared this instrument to be his/her Last Will and Testament in the presence of us and each of us, who thereupon at his/her request, in his/her presence, and in the presence of each other, have hereunto subscribed our names as witnesses thereto. We understand this to be his/her will and to the best of our knowledge testator is of legal age, of sound mind and under no constraint or undue influence.

_____residing at_____

_____residing at_____

Page _____ of _____

SELF-PROVED WILL PAGE
(attach to Will)

STATE OF ILLINOIS

COUNTY OF _____

We, _____, _____, and
_____ the testator and the witnesses respectively, whose names are signed to the attached or foregoing instrument, having been sworn, declared to the undersigned officer that the testator, in the presence of witnesses, signed the instrument as his/her last will, that he/she signed, and that each of the witnesses, in the presence of the testator and in the presence of each other, signed the will as witnesses.

_____
Testator

_____
Witness

_____
Witness

Subscribed and sworn to before me by _____ the testator, and by _____ and _____, the witnesses, all of whom personally appeared before me on _____, _____. The testator, _____ is personally known to me or has produced _____ as identification, _____ is personally known to me or has produced _____ as identification _____ is personally known to me or has produced _____ as identification.

_____
Notary Public
My commission expires:
My commission number is:

(Notary Seal)

Page _____ of _____

119

This page intentionally left blank.

Last Will and Testament

I, _____ a resident of _____ County, Illinois do hereby make, publish and declare this to be my Last Will and Testament, hereby revoking any and all Wills and Codicils heretofore made by me.

FIRST: I direct that all my just debts and funeral expenses be paid out of my estate as soon after my death as is practicable.

SECOND: I give and bequeath the following personal property unto the following persons:

_____ to _____

_____ to _____

_____ to _____

THIRD: All the rest, residue and remainder of my estate, real or personal, whereso-ever situate, now owned or hereafter acquired by me, which at the time of my death shall belong to me or be subject to my disposal by will, I give, devise and bequeath unto my spouse, _____. If my said spouse does not survive me, I give, and bequeath the said property to my children _____

_____

_____,

in equal shares or to their lineal descendants, per stirpes.

FOURTH: In the event that any beneficiary fails to survive me by thirty days, then this will shall take effect as if that person had predeceased me.

FIFTH: I hereby nominate, constitute and appoint _____ to serve as Executor of this, my Last Will and Testament, to serve without bond or surety. In the event that he or she is unable or unwilling to serve at any time or for any reason then I nominate, constitute and appoint _____ as alternate Executor also to serve without bond or surety. I give my said Executor the fullest power in all matters including the power to sell or convey real or personal property or any inter-est therein without court order.

Initials: _____ _____ _____   Page ____ of ____
            Testator   Witness   Witness

IN WITNESS WHEREOF I declare this to be my Last Will and Testament and execute it willingly as my free and voluntary act for the purposes expressed herein and I am of legal age and sound mind and make this under no constraint or undue influence, this _____ day of _____, _____.

_____

The foregoing instrument was on said date subscribed at the end thereof by _____, the above named Testator who signed, published, and declared this instrument to be his/her Last Will and Testament in the presence of us and each of us, who thereupon at his/her request, in his/her presence, and in the presence of each other, have hereunto subscribed our names as witnesses thereto. We understand this to be his/her will and to the best of our knowledge testator is of legal age, of sound mind and under no constraint or undue influence.

_____residing at_____

_____residing at_____

Page _____ of _____

SELF-PROVED WILL PAGE
(attach to Will)

STATE OF ILLINOIS

COUNTY OF _____

    We, _____, _____, and
_____ the testator and the witnesses respectively, whose names
are signed to the attached or foregoing instrument, having been sworn, declared to the
undersigned officer that the testator, in the presence of witnesses, signed the instrument as
his/her last will, that he/she signed, and that each of the witnesses, in the presence of the testator and in the presence of each other, signed the will as witnesses.

_____
Testator

_____
Witness

_____
Witness

    Subscribed and sworn to before me by _____ the testator,
and by _____ and _____, the witnesses,
all of whom personally appeared before me on _____, _____. The
testator, _____ is personally known to me or has produced
_____ as identification, _____ is per-
sonally known to me or has produced _____ as identification
_____ is personally known to me or has produced
_____ as identification.

_____
Notary Public
My commission expires:
My commission number is:

(Notary Seal)

Page ____ of ____

This page intentionally left blank.

Last Will and Testament

I, _____ a resident of _____ County, Illinois do hereby make, publish and declare this to be my Last Will and Testament, hereby revoking any and all Wills and Codicils heretofore made by me.

FIRST: I direct that all my just debts and funeral expenses be paid out of my estate as soon after my death as is practicable.

SECOND: I give and bequeath the following personal property unto the following persons:

_____ to _____

_____ to _____

_____ to _____

THIRD: All the rest, residue and remainder of my estate, real or personal, wheresoever situate, now owned or hereafter acquired by me, which at the time of my death shall belong to me or be subject to my disposal by will, I give, devise and bequeath as follows: _____% to my spouse, _____ and _____% to my children, _____

_____

_____,

in equal shares or to their lineal descendants per stirpes.

FOURTH: In the event that any beneficiary fails to survive me by thirty days, then this will shall take effect as if that person had predeceased me.

FIFTH: I hereby nominate, constitute and appoint _____ to serve as Executor of this, my Last Will and Testament, to serve without bond or surety. In the event that he or she is unable or unwilling to serve at any time or for any reason then I nominate, constitute and appoint _____ as alternate Executor also to serve without bond or surety. I give my said Executor the fullest power in all matters including the power to sell or convey real or personal property or any interest therein without court order.

Initials: _____ _____ _____   Page ____ of ____
          Testator   Witness   Witness

IN WITNESS WHEREOF I declare this to be my Last Will and Testament and execute it willingly as my free and voluntary act for the purposes expressed herein and I am of legal age and sound mind and make this under no constraint or undue influence, this _____ day of _____, _____.

_____

The foregoing instrument was on said date subscribed at the end thereof by _____, the above named Testator who signed, published, and declared this instrument to be his/her Last Will and Testament in the presence of us and each of us, who thereupon at his/her request, in his/her presence, and in the presence of each other, have hereunto subscribed our names as witnesses thereto. We understand this to be his/her will and to the best of our knowledge testator is of legal age, of sound mind and under no constraint or undue influence.

_____residing at_____

_____residing at_____

Page ____ of ____

SELF-PROVED WILL PAGE
(attach to Will)

STATE OF ILLINOIS

COUNTY OF _____

We, _____, _____, and
_____ the testator and the witnesses respectively, whose names
are signed to the attached or foregoing instrument, having been sworn, declared to the
undersigned officer that the testator, in the presence of witnesses, signed the instrument as
his/her last will, that he/she signed, and that each of the witnesses, in the presence of the testator and in the presence of each other, signed the will as witnesses.

_____
Testator

_____
Witness

_____
Witness

Subscribed and sworn to before me by _____ the testator,
and by _____ and _____, the witnesses,
all of whom personally appeared before me on _____, _____. The
testator, _____ is personally known to me or has produced
_____ as identification, _____ is per-
sonally known to me or has produced _____ as identification
_____ is personally known to me or has produced
_____ as identification.

_____
Notary Public
My commission expires:
My commission number is:

(Notary Seal)

Page _____ of _____

This page intentionally left blank.

Last Will and Testament

I, _____ a resident of _____ County, Illinois do hereby make, publish and declare this to be my Last Will and Testament, hereby revoking any and all Wills and Codicils heretofore made by me.

FIRST: I direct that all my just debts and funeral expenses be paid out of my estate as soon after my death as is practicable.

SECOND: I give and bequeath the following personal property unto the following persons:

_____ to _____

_____ to _____

_____ to _____

THIRD: All the rest, residue and remainder of my estate, real or personal, whereso-ever situate, now owned or hereafter acquired by me, which at the time of my death shall belong to me or be subject to my disposal by will, I give, devise and bequeath unto my children _____

_____

_____,

plus any afterborn or adopted children in equal shares or to their lineal descendants per stirpes.

FOURTH: In the event that any beneficiary fails to survive me by thirty days, then this will shall take effect as if that person had predeceased me.

FOURTH: In the event any of my children have not attained the age of 18 years at the time of my death, I hereby nominate, constitute and appoint _____ as guardian over the person and estate of any of my children who have not reached the age of majority at the time of my death. In the even that said guardian is unable or unwilling to serve then I nominate, constitute and appoint _____ as guardian. Said guardian to serve without bond or surety.

FIFTH: I hereby nominate, constitute and appoint _____ to serve as Executor of this, my Last Will and Testament, to serve without bond or surety. In the event that he or she is unable or unwilling to serve at any time or for any reason then I nominate, constitute and appoint _____ as alternate Executor also to serve without bond or surety. I give my said Executor the fullest power in all matters including the power to sell or convey real or personal property or any interest therein without court order.

Initials: _____ _____ _____   Page ____ of ____

　　　　　Testator　　Witness　　Witness

IN WITNESS WHEREOF I declare this to be my Last Will and Testament and execute it willingly as my free and voluntary act for the purposes expressed herein and I am of legal age and sound mind and make this under no constraint or undue influence, this _____ day of _____, _____.

_____

The foregoing instrument was on said date subscribed at the end thereof by _____, the above named Testator who signed, published, and declared this instrument to be his/her Last Will and Testament in the presence of us and each of us, who thereupon at his/her request, in his/her presence, and in the presence of each other, have hereunto subscribed our names as witnesses thereto. We understand this to be his/her will and to the best of our knowledge testator is of legal age, of sound mind and under no constraint or undue influence.

_____residing at_____

_____residing at_____

Page _____ of _____

SELF-PROVED WILL PAGE
(attach to Will)

STATE OF ILLINOIS

COUNTY OF _____

We, _____, _____, and
_____ the testator and the witnesses respectively, whose names
are signed to the attached or foregoing instrument, having been sworn, declared to the
undersigned officer that the testator, in the presence of witnesses, signed the instrument as
his/her last will, that he/she signed, and that each of the witnesses, in the presence of the testator and in the presence of each other, signed the will as witnesses.

_____
Testator

_____
Witness

_____
Witness

Subscribed and sworn to before me by _____ the testator,
and by _____ and _____, the witnesses,
all of whom personally appeared before me on _____, _____. The
testator, _____ is personally known to me or has produced
_____ as identification, _____ is personally known to me or has produced _____ as identification
_____ is personally known to me or has produced
_____ as identification.

_____
Notary Public
My commission expires:
My commission number is:

(Notary Seal)

Page ____ of ____

This page intentionally left blank.

Last Will and Testament

I, _____ a resident of _____ County, Illinois do hereby make, publish and declare this to be my Last Will and Testament, hereby revoking any and all Wills and Codicils heretofore made by me.

FIRST: I direct that all my just debts and funeral expenses be paid out of my estate as soon after my death as is practicable.

SECOND: I give and bequeath the following personal property unto the following persons:

_____ to _____
_____ to _____
_____ to _____

THIRD: All the rest, residue and remainder of my estate, real or personal, whereso-ever situate, now owned or hereafter acquired by me, which at the time of my death shall belong to me or be subject to my disposal by will, I give, devise and bequeath unto my children _____

_____

_____,
plus any afterborn or adopted children in equal shares or to their lineal descendants per stirpes.

FOURTH: In the event that any beneficiary fails to survive me by thirty days, then this will shall take effect as if that person had predeceased me.

FIFTH: In the event any of my children have not attained the age of 18 years at the time of my death, I hereby nominate, constitute and appoint _____ as guardian over the person of any of my children who have not reached the age of majority at the time of my death. In the even that said guardian is unable or unwilling to serve then I nominate, constitute and appoint _____ as guardian. Said guardian to serve without bond or surety.

SIXTH: In the event any of my children have not attained the age of 18 years at the time of my death, I hereby nominate, constitute and appoint _____ as guardian over the estate of any of my children who have not reached the age of majority at the time of my death. In the even that said guardian is unable or unwilling to serve then I nominate, constitute and appoint _____ as guardian. Said guardian to serve without bond or surety.

Initials: _____ _____ _____   Page ____ of ____
          Testator   Witness   Witness

SEVENTH: I hereby nominate, constitute and appoint _____ to serve as Executor of this, my Last Will and Testament, to serve without bond or surety. In the event that he or she is unable or unwilling to serve at any time or for any reason then I nominate, constitute and appoint _____ as alternate Executor also to serve without bond or surety. I give my said Executor the fullest power in all matters including the power to sell or convey real or personal property or any interest therein without court order.

IN WITNESS WHEREOF I declare this to be my Last Will and Testament and execute it willingly as my free and voluntary act for the purposes expressed herein and I am of legal age and sound mind and make this under no constraint or undue influence, this _____ day of _____, _____.

_____

The foregoing instrument was on said date subscribed at the end thereof by _____, the above named Testator who signed, published, and declared this instrument to be his/her Last Will and Testament in the presence of us and each of us, who thereupon at his/her request, in his/her presence, and in the presence of each other, have hereunto subscribed our names as witnesses thereto. We understand this to be his/her will and to the best of our knowledge testator is of legal age, of sound mind and under no constraint or undue influence.

_____residing at_____

_____residing at_____

Page _____ of _____

SELF-PROVED WILL PAGE
(attach to Will)

STATE OF ILLINOIS

COUNTY OF _____

We, _____, _____, and
_____ the testator and the witnesses respectively, whose names
are signed to the attached or foregoing instrument, having been sworn, declared to the
undersigned officer that the testator, in the presence of witnesses, signed the instrument as
his/her last will, that he/she signed, and that each of the witnesses, in the presence of the testator and in the presence of each other, signed the will as witnesses.

_____
Testator

_____
Witness

_____
Witness

Subscribed and sworn to before me by _____ the testator,
and by _____ and _____, the witnesses,
all of whom personally appeared before me on _____, _____. The
testator, _____ is personally known to me or has produced
_____ as identification, _____ is per-
sonally known to me or has produced _____ as identification
_____ is personally known to me or has produced
_____ as identification.

_____
Notary Public
My commission expires:
My commission number is:

(Notary Seal)

Page _____ of _____

135

This page intentionally left blank.

Last Will and Testament

I, _____ a resident of _____ County, Illinois do hereby make, publish and declare this to be my Last Will and Testament, hereby revoking any and all Wills and Codicils heretofore made by me.

FIRST: I direct that all my just debts and funeral expenses be paid out of my estate as soon after my death as is practicable.

SECOND: I give and bequeath the following personal property unto the following persons:

_____ to _____
_____ to _____
_____ to _____

THIRD: All the rest, residue and remainder of my estate, real or personal, wheresoever situate, now owned or hereafter acquired by me, which at the time of my death shall belong to me or be subject to my disposal by will, I give, devise and bequeath unto my children _____

_____

_____,

plus any afterborn or adopted children in equal shares or to their lineal descendants per stirpes.

FOURTH: In the event that any beneficiary fails to survive me by thirty days, then this will shall take effect as if that person had predeceased me.

FIFTH: In the event that any of my children have not reached the age of _____ years at the time of my death, then the share of any such child shall be held in a separate trust by _____ for such child.

The trustee shall use the income and that part of the principal of the trust as is, in the trustee's sole discretion, necessary or desirable to provide proper housing, medical care, food, clothing, entertainment and education for the trust beneficiary, considering the beneficiary's other resources. Any income that is not distributed shall be added to the principal. Additionally, the trustee shall have all powers conferred by the law of the state having jurisdiction over this trust, as well as the power to pay from the assets of the trust reasonable fees necessary to administer the trust.

The trust shall terminate when the child reaches the age specified above and the remaining assets distributed to the child, unless they have been exhausted sooner. In the event the child dies prior to the termination of the trust, then the assets shall pass to the estate of the child.

Initials: _____ _____ _____   Page ____ of ____
            Testator   Witness   Witness

The interests of the beneficiary under this trust shall not be assignable and shall be free from the claims of creditors to the full extent allowed by law.

In the event the said trustee is unable or unwilling to serve for any reason, then I nominate, constitute, and appoint _____as alternate trustee. No bond shall be required of either trustee in any jurisdiction and this trust shall be administered without court supervision as allowed by law.

SIXTH: In the event any of my children have not attained the age of 18 years at the time of my death, I hereby nominate, constitute and appoint _____ as guardian over the person and estate of any of my children who have not reached the age of majority at the time of my death. In the even that said guardian is unable or unwilling to serve then I nominate, constitute and appoint _____ as guardian. Said guardian to serve without bond or surety.

SEVENTH: I hereby nominate, constitute and appoint _____ as Executor of this, my Last Will and Testament. In the event that such named person is unable or unwilling to serve at any time or for any reason then I nominate, constitute and appoint _____ as Executor in the place and stead of the person first named herein. It is my will and I direct that my Executor shall not be required to furnish a bond for the faithful performance of his or her duties in any jurisdiction, any provision of law to the contrary notwithstanding and I give my Executor full power to administer my estate, including the power to settle claims, pay debts and sell, lease or exchange real and personal property without court order.

IN WITNESS WHEREOF I declare this to be my Last Will and Testament and execute it willingly as my free and voluntary act for the purposes expressed herein and I am of legal age and sound mind and make this under no constraint or undue influence, this _____ day of _____, _____.

_____

The foregoing instrument was on said date subscribed at the end thereof by _____, the above named Testator who signed, published, and declared this instrument to be his/her Last Will and Testament in the presence of us and each of us, who thereupon at his/her request, in his/her presence, and in the presence of each other, have hereunto subscribed our names as witnesses thereto. We understand this to be his/her will and to the best of our knowledge testator is of legal age, of sound mind and under no constraint or undue influence.

_____residing at_____

_____residing at_____

Page _____ of _____

138

SELF-PROVED WILL PAGE
(attach to Will)

STATE OF ILLINOIS

COUNTY OF _____

    We, _____, _____, and
_____ the testator and the witnesses respectively, whose names
are signed to the attached or foregoing instrument, having been sworn, declared to the
undersigned officer that the testator, in the presence of witnesses, signed the instrument as
his/her last will, that he/she signed, and that each of the witnesses, in the presence of the testator and in the presence of each other, signed the will as witnesses.

                                    _____
                                    Testator

                                    _____
                                    Witness

                                    _____
                                    Witness

    Subscribed and sworn to before me by _____ the testator,
and by _____ and _____, the witnesses,
all of whom personally appeared before me on _____, _____. The
testator, _____ is personally known to me or has produced
_____ as identification, _____ is per-
sonally known to me or has produced _____ as identification
_____ is personally known to me or has produced
_____ as identification.

                                    _____
                                    Notary Public
                                    My commission expires:
                                    My commission number is:

(Notary Seal)

                                              Page ____ of ____

This page intentionally left blank.

Last Will and Testament

I, _____ a resident of _____ County, Illinois do hereby make, publish and declare this to be my Last Will and Testament, hereby revoking any and all Wills and Codicils heretofore made by me.

FIRST: I direct that all my just debts and funeral expenses be paid out of my estate as soon after my death as is practicable.

SECOND: I give and bequeath the following personal property unto the following persons:

_____ to _____
_____ to _____
_____ to _____

THIRD: All the rest, residue and remainder of my estate, real or personal, whereso-ever situate, now owned or hereafter acquired by me, which at the time of my death shall belong to me or be subject to my disposal by will, I give, devise and bequeath unto my children _____

_____

_____,

in equal shares, or their lineal descendants per stirpes.

FOURTH: In the event that any beneficiary fails to survive me by thirty days, then this will shall take effect as if that person had predeceased me.

FIFTH: I hereby nominate, constitute and appoint _____ to serve as Executor of this, my Last Will and Testament, to serve without bond or surety. In the event that he or she is unable or unwilling to serve at any time or for any reason then I nominate, constitute and appoint _____ as alternate Executor also to serve without bond or surety. I give my said Executor the fullest power in all matters including the power to sell or convey real or personal property or any interest therein without court order.

Initials: _____ _____ _____   Page ____ of ____
            Testator   Witness   Witness

IN WITNESS WHEREOF I declare this to be my Last Will and Testament and execute it willingly as my free and voluntary act for the purposes expressed herein and I am of legal age and sound mind and make this under no constraint or undue influence, this _____ day of _____, _____.

_____

The foregoing instrument was on said date subscribed at the end thereof by _____, the above named Testator who signed, published, and declared this instrument to be his/her Last Will and Testament in the presence of us and each of us, who thereupon at his/her request, in his/her presence, and in the presence of each other, have hereunto subscribed our names as witnesses thereto. We understand this to be his/her will and to the best of our knowledge testator is of legal age, of sound mind and under no constraint or undue influence.

_____residing at_____

_____residing at_____

Page _____ of _____

SELF-PROVED WILL PAGE
(attach to Will)

STATE OF ILLINOIS

COUNTY OF _____

    We, _____, _____, and _____ the testator and the witnesses respectively, whose names are signed to the attached or foregoing instrument, having been sworn, declared to the undersigned officer that the testator, in the presence of witnesses, signed the instrument as his/her last will, that he/she signed, and that each of the witnesses, in the presence of the testator and in the presence of each other, signed the will as witnesses.

_____
Testator

_____
Witness

_____
Witness

    Subscribed and sworn to before me by _____ the testator, and by _____ and _____, the witnesses, all of whom personally appeared before me on _____, _____. The testator, _____ is personally known to me or has produced _____ as identification, _____ is personally known to me or has produced _____ as identification _____ is personally known to me or has produced _____ as identification.

_____
Notary Public
My commission expires:
My commission number is:

(Notary Seal)

Page _____ of _____

143

This page intentionally left blank.

Last Will and Testament

I, _____ a resident of _____ County, Illinois do hereby make, publish and declare this to be my Last Will and Testament, hereby revoking any and all Wills and Codicils heretofore made by me.

FIRST: I direct that all my just debts and funeral expenses be paid out of my estate as soon after my death as is practicable.

SECOND: I give and bequeath the following personal property unto the following persons:

_____ to _____
_____ to _____
_____ to _____

THIRD: All the rest, residue and remainder of my estate, real or personal, whereso-ever situate, now owned or hereafter acquired by me, which at the time of my death shall belong to me or be subject to my disposal by will, I give, devise and bequeath unto my children _____

_____

_____,

in equal shares, or their lineal descendants per capita.

FOURTH: In the event that any beneficiary fails to survive me by thirty days, then this will shall take effect as if that person had predeceased me.

FIFTH: I hereby nominate, constitute and appoint _____ to serve as Executor of this, my Last Will and Testament, to serve without bond or surety. In the event that he or she is unable or unwilling to serve at any time or for any reason then I nominate, constitute and appoint _____ as alternate Executor also to serve without bond or surety. I give my said Executor the fullest power in all matters including the power to sell or convey real or personal property or any interest therein without court order.

Initials: _____ _____ _____   Page ____ of ____
            Testator   Witness   Witness

IN WITNESS WHEREOF I declare this to be my Last Will and Testament and execute it willingly as my free and voluntary act for the purposes expressed herein and I am of legal age and sound mind and make this under no constraint or undue influence, this _____ day of _____, _____.

_____

The foregoing instrument was on said date subscribed at the end thereof by _____, the above named Testator who signed, published, and declared this instrument to be his/her Last Will and Testament in the presence of us and each of us, who thereupon at his/her request, in his/her presence, and in the presence of each other, have hereunto subscribed our names as witnesses thereto. We understand this to be his/her will and to the best of our knowledge testator is of legal age, of sound mind and under no constraint or undue influence.

_____residing at_____

_____residing at_____

Page _____ of _____

SELF-PROVED WILL PAGE
(attach to Will)

STATE OF ILLINOIS

COUNTY OF _____

We, _____, _____, and
_____ the testator and the witnesses respectively, whose names
are signed to the attached or foregoing instrument, having been sworn, declared to the
undersigned officer that the testator, in the presence of witnesses, signed the instrument as
his/her last will, that he/she signed, and that each of the witnesses, in the presence of the testator and in the presence of each other, signed the will as witnesses.

_____
Testator

_____
Witness

_____
Witness

Subscribed and sworn to before me by _____ the testator,
and by _____ and _____, the witnesses,
all of whom personally appeared before me on _____, _____. The
testator, _____ is personally known to me or has produced
_____ as identification, _____ is per-
sonally known to me or has produced _____ as identification
_____ is personally known to me or has produced
_____ as identification.

_____
Notary Public
My commission expires:
My commission number is:

(Notary Seal)

Page ____ of ____

147

This page intentionally left blank.

Last Will and Testament

I, _____ a resident of _____ County, Illinois do hereby make, publish and declare this to be my Last Will and Testament, hereby revoking any and all Wills and Codicils heretofore made by me.

FIRST: I direct that all my just debts and funeral expenses be paid out of my estate as soon after my death as is practicable.

SECOND: I give and bequeath the following personal property unto the following persons:

_____ to _____

_____ to _____

_____ to _____

THIRD: All the rest, residue and remainder of my estate, real or personal, whereso-ever situate, now owned or hereafter acquired by me, which at the time of my death shall belong to me or be subject to my disposal by will, I give, devise and bequeath unto the fol-lowing: _____

_____

_____,

or to the survivor of them.

FOURTH: In the event that any beneficiary fails to survive me by thirty days, then this will shall take effect as if that person had predeceased me.

FIFTH: I hereby nominate, constitute and appoint _____ to serve as Executor of this, my Last Will and Testament, to serve without bond or surety. In the event that he or she is unable or unwilling to serve at any time or for any reason then I nominate, constitute and appoint _____ as alternate Executor also to serve without bond or surety. I give my said Executor the fullest power in all matters including the power to sell or convey real or personal property or any inter-est therein without court order.

Initials: _____ _____ _____   Page ____ of ____
        Testator   Witness   Witness

IN WITNESS WHEREOF I declare this to be my Last Will and Testament and execute it willingly as my free and voluntary act for the purposes expressed herein and I am of legal age and sound mind and make this under no constraint or undue influence, this _____ day of _____, _____.

_____

The foregoing instrument was on said date subscribed at the end thereof by _____, the above named Testator who signed, published, and declared this instrument to be his/her Last Will and Testament in the presence of us and each of us, who thereupon at his/her request, in his/her presence, and in the presence of each other, have hereunto subscribed our names as witnesses thereto. We understand this to be his/her will and to the best of our knowledge testator is of legal age, of sound mind and under no constraint or undue influence.

_____residing at_____

_____residing at_____

Page _____ of _____

SELF-PROVED WILL PAGE
(attach to Will)

STATE OF ILLINOIS

COUNTY OF _____

    We, _____, _____, and _____ the testator and the witnesses respectively, whose names are signed to the attached or foregoing instrument, having been sworn, declared to the undersigned officer that the testator, in the presence of witnesses, signed the instrument as his/her last will, that he/she signed, and that each of the witnesses, in the presence of the testator and in the presence of each other, signed the will as witnesses.

_____

Testator

_____

Witness

_____

Witness

    Subscribed and sworn to before me by _____ the testator, and by _____ and _____, the witnesses, all of whom personally appeared before me on _____, _____. The testator, _____ is personally known to me or has produced _____ as identification, _____ is personally known to me or has produced _____ as identification _____ is personally known to me or has produced _____ as identification.

_____

Notary Public
My commission expires:
My commission number is:

(Notary Seal)

Page ____ of ____

This page intentionally left blank.

Last Will and Testament

I, _____ a resident of _____
County, Illinois do hereby make, publish and declare this to be my Last Will and Testament,
hereby revoking any and all Wills and Codicils heretofore made by me.

FIRST: I direct that all my just debts and funeral expenses be paid out of my estate as
soon after my death as is practicable.

SECOND: I give and bequeath the following personal property unto the following
persons:

_____ to _____
_____ to _____
_____ to _____

THIRD: All the rest, residue and remainder of my estate, real or personal, whereso-
ever situate, now owned or hereafter acquired by me, which at the time of my death shall
belong to me or be subject to my disposal by will, I give, devise and bequeath unto the following _____
_____
_____,
in equal shares, or their lineal descendants per stirpes.

FOURTH: In the event that any beneficiary fails to survive me by thirty days, then
this will shall take effect as if that person had predeceased me.

FIFTH: I hereby nominate, constitute and appoint _____ to
serve as Executor of this, my Last Will and Testament, to serve without bond or surety.
In the event that he or she is unable or unwilling to serve at any time or for any reason
then I nominate, constitute and appoint _____ as alternate
Executor also to serve without bond or surety. I give my said Executor the fullest power
in all matters including the power to sell or convey real or personal property or any interest therein without court order.

Initials: _____ _____ _____   Page ____ of ____
        Testator   Witness   Witness

IN WITNESS WHEREOF I declare this to be my Last Will and Testament and execute it willingly as my free and voluntary act for the purposes expressed herein and I am of legal age and sound mind and make this under no constraint or undue influence, this _____ day of _____, _____.

_____

The foregoing instrument was on said date subscribed at the end thereof by _____, the above named Testator who signed, published, and declared this instrument to be his/her Last Will and Testament in the presence of us and each of us, who thereupon at his/her request, in his/her presence, and in the presence of each other, have hereunto subscribed our names as witnesses thereto. We understand this to be his/her will and to the best of our knowledge testator is of legal age, of sound mind and under no constraint or undue influence.

_____residing at_____

_____residing at_____

Page _____ of _____

SELF-PROVED WILL PAGE
(attach to Will)

STATE OF ILLINOIS

COUNTY OF _____

We, _____, _____, and _____ the testator and the witnesses respectively, whose names are signed to the attached or foregoing instrument, having been sworn, declared to the undersigned officer that the testator, in the presence of witnesses, signed the instrument as his/her last will, that he/she signed, and that each of the witnesses, in the presence of the testator and in the presence of each other, signed the will as witnesses.

_____
Testator

_____
Witness

_____
Witness

Subscribed and sworn to before me by _____ the testator, and by _____ and _____, the witnesses, all of whom personally appeared before me on _____, _____. The testator, _____ is personally known to me or has produced _____ as identification, _____ is personally known to me or has produced _____ as identification _____ is personally known to me or has produced _____ as identification.

_____
Notary Public
My commission expires:
My commission number is:

(Notary Seal)

Page ____ of ____

This page intentionally left blank.

Codicil to the Will of

_____

I, _____, a resident of _____ County, Illinois declare this to be the first codicil to my Last Will and Testament dated _____, _____.

FIRST: I hereby revoke the clause of my Will which reads as follows: _____
_____
_____
_____

SECOND: I hereby add following clause to my Will: _____
_____
_____
_____

THIRD: In all other respects I hereby confirm and republish my Last Will and Testament dated _____, _____.

Date: _____   _____

We, the undersigned persons, of lawful age, have on this _____ day of _____, _____, at the request of _____, witnessed his/her signature to the foregoing First Codicil to Will in the presence of each of us; and we have, at the same time and in his/her presence and in the presence of each other, subscribed our names hereto as attesting witnesses.

_____ residing at: _____
                                               _____

_____ residing at: _____
                                               _____

SELF-PROVING AFFIDAVIT

STATE OF ILLINOIS   §
                                     §
COUNTY OF _____   §

We, _____ and _____ and _____, the testator and the witnesses, whose names are signed to the attached or foregoing instrument in those capacities, personally appearing before the undersigned authority and being first duly sworn, declare to the undersigned authority under penalty of perjury that: 1) the testator declared, signed and executed the instrument as his or her last will; 2) he or she signed it willingly or directed another to sign for him or her; 3) he or she executed it as his or her free and voluntary act for the purposes therein expressed; and 4) each of the witnesses, and the request of the testator, in his or her hearing and presence and in the presence of each other, signed the will as witnesses and that to the best of his or her knowledge the testator was at that time of full legal age, of sound mind and under no constraint or undue influence.

_____   _____
TESTATOR   WITNESS

                                           _____
                                           WITNESS

SUBSCRIBED AND ACKNOWLEDGED before me by _____, the Testator and subscribed and sworn to before me by the above-named witnesses this _____ day of_____, _____.

                                           _____
                                           Notary Public

Page _____ of _____

157

This page intentionally left blank.

LIVING WILL DECLARATION

This declaration is made this _____ day of _____ (month, year).

I, _____, being of sound mind, willfully and voluntarily make known my desires that my moment of death shall not be artificially postponed.

If at any time I should have an incurable and irreversible injury, disease, or illness judged to be a terminal condition by my attending physician who has personally examined me and has determined that my death is imminent except for death delaying procedures, I direct that such procedures which would only prolong the dying process be withheld or withdrawn, and that I be permitted to die naturally with only the administration of medication, sustenance, or the performance of any medical procedure deemed necessary by my attending physician to provide me with comfort care.

In the absence of my ability to give directions regarding the use of such death delaying procedures, it is my intention that this declaration shall be honored by my family and physician as the final expression of my legal right to refuse medical or surgical treatment and accept the consequences from such refusal.

Signed _____

City, County and State of Residence _____

The declarant is personally known to me and I believe him or her to be of sound mind. I saw the declarant sign the declaration in my presence (or the declarant acknowledged in my presence that he or she had signed the declaration) and I signed the declaration as a witness in the presence of the declarant. I did not sign the declarant's signature above for or at the direction of the declarant. At the date of this instrument, I am not entitled to any portion of the estate of the declarant according to the laws of intestate succession or, to the best of my knowledge and belief, under any will or declarant or other instrument taking effect at declarant's death, or directly financially responsible for declarant's medical care.

Witness _____

Witness _____

This page intentionally left blank.

Illinois Statutory Short Form Power of Attorney for Health Care

(NOTICE: THE PURPOSE OF THIS POWER OF ATTORNEY IS TO GIVE THE PERSON YOU DESIGNATE (YOUR "AGENT") BROAD POWERS TO MAKE HEALTH CARE DECISIONS FOR YOU, INCLUDING POWER TO REQUIRE, CONSENT TO OR WITHDRAW ANY TYPE OF PERSONAL CARE OR MEDICAL TREATMENT FOR ANY PHYSICAL OR MENTAL CONDITION AND TO ADMIT YOU TO OR DISCHARGE YOU FROM ANY HOSPITAL, HOME OR OTHER INSTITUTION. THIS FORM DOES NOT IMPOSE A DUTY ON YOUR AGENT TO EXERCISE GRANTED POWERS; BUT WHEN POWERS ARE EXERCISED, YOUR AGENT WILL HAVE TO USE DUE CARE TO ACT FOR YOUR BENEFIT AND IN ACCORDANCE WITH THIS FORM AND KEEP A RECORD OF RECEIPTS, DISBURSEMENTS AND SIGNIFICANT ACTIONS TAKEN AS AGENT. A COURT CAN TAKE AWAY THE POWERS OF YOUR AGENT IF IT FINDS THE AGENT IS NOT ACTING PROPERLY. YOU MAY NAME SUCCESSOR AGENTS UNDER THIS FORM BUT NOT CO-AGENTS, AND NO HEALTH CARE PROVIDER MAY BE NAMED. UNLESS YOU EXPRESSLY LIMIT THE DURATION OF THIS POWER IN THE MANNER PROVIDED BELOW, UNTIL YOU REVOKE THIS POWER OR A COURT ACTING ON YOUR BEHALF TERMINATES IT, YOUR AGENT MAY EXERCISE THE POWERS GIVEN HERE THROUGHOUT YOUR LIFETIME, EVEN AFTER YOU BECOME DISABLED. THE POWERS YOU GIVE YOUR AGENT, YOUR RIGHT TO REVOKE THOSE POWERS AND THE PENALTIES FOR VIOLATING THE LAW ARE EXPLAINED MORE FULLY IN SECTIONS 4-5, 4-6, 4-9 AND 4-10(b) OF THE ILLINOIS "POWERS OF ATTORNEY FOR HEALTH CARE LAW" OF WHICH THIS FORM IS A PART (SEE THE BACK OF THIS FORM). THAT LAW EXPRESSLY PERMITS THE USE OF ANY DIFFERENT FORM OF POWER OF ATTORNEY YOU MAY DESIRE. IF THERE IS ANYTHING ABOUT THIS FORM THAT YOU DO NOT UNDERSTAND, YOU SHOULD ASK A LAWYER TO EXPLAIN IT TO YOU.)

POWER OF ATTORNEY made this _____ day of _____
(month)   (year)

1. I, _____

_____
(insert name and address of principal)

hereby appoint:

_____

_____
(insert name and address of agent)

as my attorney-in-fact (my "agent") to act for me and in my name (in any way I could act in person) to make any and all decisions for me concerning my personal care, medical treatment, hospitalization and health care and to require, withhold or withdraw any type of medical treatment or procedure, even though my death may ensue. My agent shall have the same access to my medical records that I have, including the right to disclose the contents to others. My agent shall also have full power to make a disposition of any part or all of my body for medical purposes, authorize an autopsy and direct the disposition of my remains.

(THE ABOVE GRANT OF POWER IS INTENDED TO BE AS BROAD AS POSSIBLE SO THAT YOUR AGENT WILL HAVE AUTHORITY TO MAKE ANY DECISION YOU COULD MAKE TO OBTAIN OR TERMINATE ANY TYPE OF HEALTH CARE, INCLUDING WITHDRAWAL OF FOOD AND WATER AND OTHER LIFE-SUSTAINING MEASURES, IF YOUR AGENT BELIEVES SUCH ACTION WOULD BE CONSISTENT WITH YOUR INTENT AND DESIRES. IF YOU WISH TO LIMIT THE SCOPE OF YOUR AGENT'S POWERS OR PRESCRIBE SPECIAL RULES OR LIMIT THE POWER TO MAKE AN ANATOMICAL GIFT, AUTHORIZE AUTOPSY OR DISPOSE OF REMAINS, YOU MAY DO SO IN THE FOLLOWING PARAGRAPHS.)

2. The powers granted above shall not include the following powers or shall be subject to the following rules or limitations (here you may include any specific limitations you deem appropriate, such as: your own definition of when life-sustaining measures should be withheld; a direction to continue food and fluids or life-sustaining treatment in all events; or instructions to refuse any specific types of treatment that are inconsistent with your religious beliefs or unacceptable to you for any other reason, such as blood transfusion, electro-convulsive therapy, amputation, psychosurgery, voluntary admission to a mental institution, etc.):

_____

_____

(THE SUBJECT OF LIFE-SUSTAINING TREATMENT IS OF PARTICULAR IMPORTANCE. FOR YOUR CONVENIENCE IN DEALING WITH THAT SUBJECT, SOME GENERAL STATEMENTS CONCERNING THE WITHHOLDING OR REMOVAL OF LIFE-SUSTAINING TREATMENT ARE SET FORTH BELOW. IF YOU AGREE WITH ONE OF THESE STATEMENTS, YOU MAY INITIAL THAT STATEMENT; BUT DO NOT INITIAL MORE THAN ONE):

I do not want my life to be prolonged nor do I want life-sustaining treatment to be provided or continued if my agent believes the burdens of the treatment outweigh the expected benefits. I want my agent to consider the relief of suffering, the expense involved and the quality as well as the possible extension of my life in making decisions concerning life sustaining treatment.

Initialed _____

Page ____ of ____

I want my life to be prolonged and I want life-sustaining treatment to be provided or continued unless I am in a coma which my attending physician believes to be irreversible, in accordance with reasonable medical standards at the time of reference. If and when I have suffered irreversible coma, I want life-sustaining treatment to be withheld or discontinued.

Initialed _____

I want my life to be prolonged to the greatest extent possible without regard to my condition, the chances I have for recovery or the cost of the procedures.

Initialed _____

(THIS POWER OF ATTORNEY MAY BE AMENDED OR REVOKED BY YOU IN THE MANNER PROVIDED IN SECTION 4-6 OF THE ILLINOIS "POWERS OF ATTORNEY FOR HEALTH CARE LAW" (SEE THE BACK OF THIS FORM). ABSENT AMENDMENT OR REVOCATION, THE AUTHORITY GRANTED IN THIS POWER OF ATTORNEY WILL BECOME EFFECTIVE AT THE TIME THIS POWER IS SIGNED AND WILL CONTINUE UNTIL YOUR DEATH, AND BEYOND IF ANATOMICAL GIFT, AUTOPSY OR DISPOSITION OF REMAINS IS AUTHORIZED, UNLESS A LIMITATION ON THE BEGINNING DATE OR DURATION IS MADE BY INITIALING AND COMPLETING EITHER OR BOTH OF THE FOLLOWING:)

3. (_____) This power of attorney shall become effective on _____
_____(insert a future date or event during your lifetime, such as court determination of your disability, when you want this power to first take effect)

4. (_____) This power of attorney shall terminate on_____
_____(insert a future date or event, such as court determination of your disability, when you want this power to terminate prior to your death)

(IF YOU WISH TO NAME SUCCESSOR AGENTS, INSERT THE NAMES AND ADDRESSES OF SUCH SUCCESSORS IN THE FOLLOWING PARAGRAPH.)

5. If any agent named by me shall die, become incompetent, resign, refuse to accept the office of agent or be unavailable, I name the following (each to act alone and successively, in the order named) as successors to such agent:_____
_____

For purposes of this paragraph 5, a person shall be considered to be incompetent if and while the person is a minor or an adjudicated incompetent or disabled person or the person is unable to give prompt and intelligent consideration to health care matters, as certified by a licensed physician.

(IF YOU WISH TO NAME YOUR AGENT AS GUARDIAN OF YOUR PERSON, IN THE EVENT A COURT DECIDES THAT ONE SHOULD BE APPOINTED, YOU MAY, BUT ARE NOT REQUIRED TO, DO SO BY RETAINING THE FOLLOWING PARAGRAPH. THE COURT WILL APPOINT YOUR AGENT IF THE COURT FINDS THAT SUCH APPOINTMENT WILL SERVE YOUR BEST INTERESTS AND WELFARE. STRIKE OUT PARAGRAPH 6 IF YOU DO NOT WANT YOUR AGENT TO ACT AS GUARDIAN.)

6. If a guardian of my person is to be appointed, I nominate the agent acting under this power of attorney as such guardian, to serve without bond or security. (insert name and address of nominated guardian of the person)

7. I am fully informed as to all the contents of this form and understand the full import of this grant of powers to my agent.

Signed _____
(principal)

The principal has had an opportunity to read the above form and has signed the form or acknowledged his or her signature or mark on the form in my presence.

_____   Residing at _____
(witness)   _____

(YOU MAY, BUT ARE NOT REQUIRED TO, REQUEST YOUR AGENT AND SUCCESSOR AGENTS TO PROVIDE SPECIMEN SIGNATURES BELOW. IF YOU INCLUDE SPECIMEN SIGNATURES IN THIS POWER OF ATTORNEY YOU MUST COMPLETE THE CERTIFICATION OPPOSITE THE SIGNATURES OF THE AGENTS.)

Specimen signatures of agent (and successors).   I certify that the signatures of my agent (and successors) are correct

_____   _____
(agent)   (principal)

_____   _____
(successor agent)   (principal)

_____   _____
(successor agent)   (principal)

UNIFORM DONOR CARD

The undersigned hereby makes this anatomical gift, if medically acceptable, to take effect on death. The words and marks below indicate my desires:

I give:

        (a) _____ any needed organs or parts;

        (b) _____ only the following organs or parts

_____

for the purpose of transplantation, therapy, medical research, or education;

        (c) _____ my body for anatomical study if needed.

Limitations or special wishes, if any:

_____

Signed by the donor and the following witnesses in the presence of each other:

_____ _____
Signature of Donor   Date of birth

_____ _____
Date signed   City & State

_____ _____
Witness   Witness

_____ _____
Address   Address

UNIFORM DONOR CARD

The undersigned hereby makes this anatomical gift, if medically acceptable, to take effect on death. The words and marks below indicate my desires:

I give:

        (a) _____ any needed organs or parts;

        (b) _____ only the following organs or parts

_____

for the purpose of transplantation, therapy, medical research, or education;

        (c) _____ my body for anatomical study if needed.

Limitations or special wishes, if any:

_____

Signed by the donor and the following witnesses in the presence of each other:

_____ _____
Signature of Donor   Date of birth

_____ _____
Date signed   City & State

_____ _____
Witness   Witness

_____ _____
Address   Address

UNIFORM DONOR CARD

The undersigned hereby makes this anatomical gift, if medically acceptable, to take effect on death. The words and marks below indicate my desires:

I give:

        (a) _____ any needed organs or parts;

        (b) _____ only the following organs or parts

_____

for the purpose of transplantation, therapy, medical research, or education;

        (c) _____ my body for anatomical study if needed.

Limitations or special wishes, if any:

_____

Signed by the donor and the following witnesses in the presence of each other:

_____ _____
Signature of Donor   Date of birth

_____ _____
Date signed   City & State

_____ _____
Witness   Witness

_____ _____
Address   Address

UNIFORM DONOR CARD

The undersigned hereby makes this anatomical gift, if medically acceptable, to take effect on death. The words and marks below indicate my desires:

I give:

        (a) _____ any needed organs or parts;

        (b) _____ only the following organs or parts

_____

for the purpose of transplantation, therapy, medical research, or education;

        (c) _____ my body for anatomical study if needed.

Limitations or special wishes, if any:

_____

Signed by the donor and the following witnesses in the presence of each other:

_____ _____
Signature of Donor   Date of birth

_____ _____
Date signed   City & State

_____ _____
Witness   Witness

_____ _____
Address   Address

One of these cards should be cut out and carried in your wallet or purse.

INDEX

SPHINX® PUBLISHING ORDER FORM

Qty	ISBN	Title	Retail	Ext.
		SPHINX PUBLISHING NATIONAL TITLES		
____	1-57248-148-X	Cómo Hacer su Propio Testamento	$16.95	____
____	1-57248-147-1	Cómo Solicitar su Propio Divorcio	$24.95	____
____	1-57248-166-8	The Complete Book of Corporate Forms	$24.95	____
____	1-57248-163-3	Crime Victim's Guide to Justice (2E)	$21.95	____
____	1-57248-159-5	Essential Guide to Real Estate Contracts	$18.95	____
____	1-57248-160-9	Essential Guide to Real Estate Leases	$18.95	____
____	1-57248-139-0	Grandparents' Rights (3E)	$24.95	____
____	1-57248-188-9	Guía de Inmigración a Estados Unidos (3E)	$24.95	____
____	1-57248-187-0	Guía de Justicia para Víctimas del Crimen	$21.95	____
____	1-57248-103-X	Help Your Lawyer Win Your Case (2E)	$14.95	____
____	1-57248-164-1	How to Buy a Condominium or Townhome (2E)	$19.95	____
____	1-57248-191-9	How to File Your Own Bankruptcy (5E)	$21.95	____
____	1-57248-132-3	How to File Your Own Divorce (4E)	$24.95	____
____	1-57248-100-5	How to Form a DE Corporation from Any State	$24.95	____
____	1-57248-083-1	How to Form a Limited Liability Company	$22.95	____
____	1-57248-099-8	How to Form a Nonprofit Corporation	$24.95	____
____	1-57248-133-1	How to Form Your Own Corporation (3E)	$24.95	____
____	1-57071-343-X	How to Form Your Own Partnership	$22.95	____
____	1-57248-119-6	How to Make Your Own Will (2E)	$16.95	____
____	1-57248-124-2	How to Register Your Own Copyright (3E)	$21.95	____
____	1-57248-104-8	How to Register Your Own Trademark (3E)	$21.95	____
____	1-57071-349-9	How to Win Your Unemployment Compensation Claim	$21.95	____
____	1-57248-118-8	How to Write Your Own Living Will (2E)	$16.95	____
____	1-57071-344-8	How to Write Your Own Premarital Agreement (2E)	$21.95	____
____	1-57248-158-7	Incorporate in Nevada from Any State	$24.95	____
____	1-57071-333-2	Jurors' Rights (2E)	$12.95	____
____	1-57071-400-2	Legal Research Made Easy (2E)	$16.95	____
____	1-57071-336-7	Living Trusts and Simple Ways to Avoid Probate (2E)	$22.95	____

Qty	ISBN	Title	Retail	Ext.
____	1-57248-186-2	Manual de Beneficios para el Seguro Social	$18.95	____
____	1-57248-167-6	Most Valuable Bus. Legal Forms You'll Ever Need (3E)	$21.95	____
____	1-57248-130-7	Most Valuable Personal Legal Forms You'll Ever Need	$24.95	____
____	1-57248-098-X	The Nanny and Domestic Help Legal Kit	$22.95	____
____	1-57248-089-0	Neighbor v. Neighbor (2E)	$16.95	____
____	1-57071-348-0	The Power of Attorney Handbook (3E)	$19.95	____
____	1-57248-149-8	Repair Your Own Credit and Deal with Debt	$18.95	____
____	1-57248-168-4	The Social Security Benefits Handbook (3E)	$18.95	____
____	1-57071-399-5	Unmarried Parents' Rights	$19.95	____
____	1-57071-354-5	U.S.A. Immigration Guide (3E)	$19.95	____
____	1-57248-138-2	Winning Your Personal Injury Claim (2E)	$24.95	____
____	1-57248-162-5	Your Right to Child Custody, Visitation and Support (2E)	$24.95	____
____	1-57248-157-9	Your Rights When You Owe Too Much	$16.95	____
		CALIFORNIA TITLES		
____	1-57248-150-1	CA Power of Attorney Handbook (2E)	$18.95	____
____	1-57248-151-X	How to File for Divorce in CA (3E)	$26.95	____
____	1-57071-356-1	How to Make a CA Will	$16.95	____
____	1-57248-145-5	How to Probate and Settle an Estate in California	$26.95	____
____	1-57248-146-3	How to Start a Business in CA	$18.95	____
____	1-57071-358-8	How to Win in Small Claims Court in CA	$16.95	____
____	1-57071-359-6	Landlords' Rights and Duties in CA	$21.95	____
		FLORIDA TITLES		
____	1-57071-363-4	Florida Power of Attorney Handbook (2E)	$16.95	____
____	1-57248-176-5	How to File for Divorce in FL (7E)	$26.95	____
____	1-57248-177-3	How to Form a Corporation in FL (5E)	$24.95	____
____	1-57248-086-6	How to Form a Limited Liability Co. in FL	$22.95	____
____	1-57071-401-0	How to Form a Partnership in FL	$22.95	____
____	1-57248-113-7	How to Make a FL Will (6E)	$16.95	____

Form Continued on Following Page   **SUBTOTAL**

To order, call Sourcebooks at 1-800-432-7444 or FAX (630) 961-2168 (Bookstores, libraries, wholesalers—please call for discount)

Prices are subject to change without notice.

SPHINX® PUBLISHING ORDER FORM

Qty	ISBN	Title	Retail	Ext.
	1-57248-088-2	How to Modify Your FL Divorce Judgment (4E)	$24.95	
	1-57248-144-7	How to Probate and Settle an Estate in FL (4E)	$26.95	
	1-57248-081-5	How to Start a Business in FL (5E)	$16.95	
	1-57071-362-6	How to Win in Small Claims Court in FL (6E)	$16.95	
	1-57248-123-4	Landlords' Rights and Duties in FL (8E)	$21.95	
		GEORGIA TITLES		
	1-57248-137-4	How to File for Divorce in GA (4E)	$21.95	
	1-57248-075-0	How to Make a GA Will (3E)	$16.95	
	1-57248-140-4	How to Start a Business in Georgia (2E)	$16.95	
		ILLINOIS TITLES		
	1-57071-405-3	How to File for Divorce in IL (2E)	$21.95	
	1-57248-170-6	How to Make an IL Will (3E)	$16.95	
	1-57071-416-9	How to Start a Business in IL (2E)	$18.95	
	1-57248-078-5	Landlords' Rights & Duties in IL	$21.95	
		MASSACHUSETTS TITLES		
	1-57248-128-5	How to File for Divorce in MA (3E)	$24.95	
	1-57248-115-3	How to Form a Corporation in MA	$24.95	
	1-57248-108-0	How to Make a MA Will (2E)	$16.95	
	1-57248-106-4	How to Start a Business in MA (2E)	$18.95	
	1-57248-107-2	Landlords' Rights and Duties in MA (2E)	$21.95	
		MICHIGAN TITLES		
	1-57071-409-6	How to File for Divorce in MI (2E)	$21.95	
	1-57248-077-7	How to Make a MI Will (2E)	$16.95	
	1-57071-407-X	How to Start a Business in MI (2E)	$16.95	
		MINNESOTA TITLES		
	1-57248-142-0	How to File for Divorce in MN	$21.95	
	1-57248-179-X	How to Form a Corporation in MN	$24.95	
	1-57248-178-1	How to Make a MN Will (2E)	$16.95	
		NEW YORK TITLES		
	1-57248-141-2	How to File for Divorce in NY (2E)	$26.95	
	1-57248-105-6	How to Form a Corporation in NY	$24.95	
	1-57248-095-5	How to Make a NY Will (2E)	$16.95	
	1-57071-185-2	How to Start a Business in NY	$18.95	
	1-57071-187-9	How to Win in Small Claims Court in NY	$16.95	
	1-57071-186-0	Landlords' Rights and Duties in NY	$21.95	

Qty	ISBN	Title	Retail	Ext.
	1-57071-188-7	New York Power of Attorney Handbook	$19.95	
	1-57248-122-6	Tenants' Rights in NY	$21.95	
		NORTH CAROLINA TITLES		
	1-57248-185-4	How to File for Divorce in NC (3E)	$22.95	
	1-57248-129-3	How to Make a NC Will (3E)	$16.95	
	1-57248-184-6	How to Start a Business in NC (3E)	$18.95	
	1-57248-091-2	Landlords' Rights & Duties in NC	$21.95	
		OHIO TITLES		
	1-57248-190-0	How to File for Divorce in OH (2E)	$24.95	
	1-57248-174-9	How to Form a Corporation in OH	$24.95	
	1-57248-173-0	How to Make an OH Will	$16.95	
		PENNSYLVANIA TITLES		
	1-57248-127-7	How to File for Divorce in PA (2E)	$24.95	
	1-57248-094-7	How to Make a PA Will (2E)	$16.95	
	1-57248-112-9	How to Start a Business in PA (2E)	$18.95	
	1-57071-179-8	Landlords' Rights and Duties in PA	$19.95	
		TEXAS TITLES		
	1-57248-171-4	Child Custody, Visitation, and Support in TX	$22.95	
	1-57071-330-8	How to File for Divorce in TX (2E)	$21.95	
	1-57248-114-5	How to Form a Corporation in TX (2E)	$24.95	
	1-57071-417-7	How to Make a TX Will (2E)	$16.95	
	1-57071-418-5	How to Probate an Estate in TX (2E)	$22.95	
	1-57071-365-0	How to Start a Business in TX (2E)	$18.95	
	1-57248-111-0	How to Win in Small Claims Court in TX (2E)	$16.95	
	1-57248-110-2	Landlords' Rights and Duties in TX (2E)	$21.95	

SUBTOTAL THIS PAGE _____

SUBTOTAL PREVIOUS PAGE _____

Shipping — $5.00 for 1st book, $1.00 each additional _____

Illinois residents add 6.75% sales tax _____

Connecticut residents add 6.00% sales tax _____

TOTAL _____

To order, call Sourcebooks at 1-800-432-7444 or FAX (630) 961-2168 (Bookstores, libraries, wholesalers—please call for discount)

Prices are subject to change without notice.